D0436239

DISCARDED FROM
GARFIELD COUNTY PUBLIC
LIBRARY SYSTEM

Garfield County Libraries
Glenwood Springs Branch Library
413 9th Street
Glenwood Springs, CO 81601
(970) 945-5958 Fax (970) 945-7723
www.garfieldlibraries.org

# One Simple Act

# Debbie Macomber

## One Simple Act

### Discovering the Power of Generosity

**HOWARD BOOKS**
A DIVISION OF SIMON & SCHUSTER, INC.
New York  Nashville  London  Toronto  Sydney

Published by Howard Books, a division of Simon & Schuster, Inc.
1230 Avenue of the Americas, New York, NY 10020
www.howardpublishing.com

*One Simple Act* © 2009 Debbie Macomber

All rights reserved, including the right to reproduce this book or portions thereof in any form whatsoever. For information, address Howard Subsidiary Rights Department, 1230 Avenue of the Americas, New York, NY 10020.

HOWARD and colophon are registered trademarks of Simon & Schuster, Inc.

Published in association with the Books & Such Literary Agency, 52 Mission Circle, Suite 122, PMB 170, Santa Rosa, CA 95409-5370, www.booksandsuch.biz.

Library of Congress Cataloging-in-Publication Data

Macomber, Debbie.
One simple act / Debbie Macomber.
p. cm.
1. Generosity—religious aspects—Christianity.  I. Title.
BV4647.G45M33 2009
241'.4—dc22                            2009030449
ISBN 978-1-4391-0893-2
ISBN 978-1-4391-6697-0 (ebook)
10  9  8  7  6  5  4  3  2  1

Manufactured in the United States of America

For information regarding special discounts for bulk purchases, please contact Simon & Schuster Special Sales at 1-866-506-1949 or business@simonandschuster.com.

The Simon & Schuster Speakers Bureau can bring authors to your live event. For more information or to book an event, contact the Simon & Schuster Speakers Bureau at 1-866-248-3049 or visit our Web site at www.simonspeakers.com.

Edited by Cindy Lambert
Interior Design by Jessica Shatan Heslin/Studio Shatan, Inc.

Scripture quotations not otherwise marked are taken from the *Holy Bible, New International Version* ®. Copyright © 1973, 1978, 1984 by International Bible Society. Used by permission of Zondervan. All rights reserved. Scripture quotations marked *The Message* are taken from *The Message*. Copyright © 1993, 1994, 1995, 1996, 2000, 2001, 2002. Used by permission of NavPress Publishing Group.

To my incredible Aunt Betty Stierwalt,
who is celebrating her hundredth birthday.
Her example of generosity and love
inspires all who know her.

# Contents

# *One Simple Act*.

*Give thanks in all circumstances,*

*for this is God's will for you in Christ Jesus.*

1 Thessalonians 5:18

# One

# Fleas, Footsteps, and Checkout Lanes

## The Springboard of Gratitude

Kate stepped out of her bookstore at the end of a long, tiring day, locked the door behind her, pulled her scarf up over her nose and mouth to shield her lungs from the bitter cold air, and rushed across the lot to her car. Just one quick stop at the grocery store and she'd be on the way home to cuddle up with her new book in front of a warm fire.

As she waited at the traffic light to turn into the grocery store lot, she took off one glove to feel if the air blasting out of the heat vents was starting to warm. Ah, yes. What a relief. In the few minutes it had taken her to get from her bookstore to the grocery store, her fingers had started to ache from the cold. "I think I was born with cold fingers," she muttered. The light changed to green, and as she turned into the lot she came alongside a narrow median strip and noticed a man holding a crudely made hand-lettered cardboard sign: HOMELESS. NEED FOOD. PLEASE HELP. At his feet was a small white plastic bucket. His collar was pulled high against the cold, but her eyes went to his hands holding the sign. Bare hands.

*My fingers ache from five minutes in this cold car, with gloves on. How cold must his be?* she wondered. Her eyes went to his face. *Late twenties, probably six or seven years older than Mark.* The sudden thought of her son instantly made her shoulders sag. She hadn't seen Mark since summer. Addicted to drugs, Mark had left home several months ago after a two-year struggle—maybe *war* was a better word—with his parents over his drug abuse. He still called sometimes, but he'd been bunking with friends, house hopping, and he'd even slept on the streets rather than come back home. Never had she felt so helpless as she'd felt watching her son self-destruct during these past two years, never so powerless to meet the deep needs of the son she loved. But he wasn't ready to give up his drugs or his illusion of freedom. He remained elusive about his whereabouts and declined every offer Kate made to meet him someplace to talk. *Where is he tonight? Cold and hungry like this guy? Begging on some street corner? And if a kind stranger gives him a ten-dollar bill, he'll buy his next hit of pills before buying a warm meal.* Kate's heart sank. *Are Mark's hands cold tonight?*

And then it came to her. A quiet nudge. She parked, hurried into the store to pick up bread, eggs, and some yogurt for the weekend, then hit one more aisle. Through the checkout, a dash back to her car, and back along the other side of the median strip, where she pulled alongside the young man, rolled down her window, and stopped. Her heart picked up its pace. He walked over to her car, bucket held out, but she didn't hand any money out the window.

Instead she held out a warm pair of gloves she'd just bought. He looked startled.

"Your hands must be terribly cold," she said. "I hope these help." The young man looked confused for a moment, then accepted the gloves. "Thanks," he said.

The car behind her honked and she pulled away and moved toward the intersection. She glanced in the rearview mirror and saw him pulling on the gloves. She blinked to clear a few tears away. They were warm on her cold cheeks, but another warmth from somewhere in her core was spreading upward, and she found herself smiling.

For the first time in a long time she didn't feel powerless at the thought of Mark. *Take care of my son tonight, Lord*, she prayed. *Show him Your love through the kindness of a stranger. And Lord, comfort the mother of that young man tonight.*

In that one simple act Kate had discovered the power of generosity. She'd not only warmed a troubled young man, she'd kindled a spark of hope for Mark. And she realized that God had just used her to care for the son of another worried mother. Who knows, maybe the young man on the median strip called his mother that night.

Just one simple act.

## A Discovery Worth Sharing

You've read the subtitle of this book, *Discovering the Power of Generosity*. If you recognized my name on the cover of the book you may be asking yourself why a writer known for fiction is writing a nonfiction book on generosity. The answer is . . . well . . . if you don't mind me quoting the title . . . *simple*. Have you ever discovered something so great that you just had to tell your friends? You know, like a great little vacation spot you stumbled across while on a trip, or a new clothing store with affordable prices, great selection, and really stellar service? Maybe you've heard a speaker who had a huge impact on you or saw a movie that made you laugh till you cried and you knew just the friend who needed it. When we find something we love, we want to share it with others and spread the joy. Right? That is how I feel about simple acts of generosity. I have had some encounters with generosity—as the recipient, the giver, the witness—that have had a profoundly life-changing impact on me. I've just got to share the news.

On the other hand, you may have seen the word "generosity" and thought to yourself, *Oh, great. One more appeal to go digging deep into my pocket.* Don't worry! You are not in for a brand-new load of guilt, I promise! That's precisely what this book is *not* about. In our age of overwork and exhaustion, tossing a few dollars here and there may be the easiest way to practice generosity. But I am talking about it in larger terms—life-changing terms.

Like my friend Kate. She made a five-minute investment of time and on a whim probably spent about eight or nine dollars on that pair of gloves. But her decision had nothing to do with her wallet. It had to do with her heart. When she handed those gloves out the window she brought unexpected goodness into a bleak situation. And that goodness spilled over and gave back. It multiplied. For my friend Kate, that was just the beginning. But that is a story for another time.

When you pick up a book, it's fair to ask, "What's in it for me?" My goal in writing this is to surprise you with the multiple benefits that come from small and large acts of generosity. I'm convinced that we cannot become all we could be until we are willing to unclench our hands and release what we've been clinging to, what we've been determined to keep for ourselves. The intriguing part is that once we release such gifts we are free to take hold of something more, something better, something that God has wanted to give us for a very long time.

Simply put, intentional acts of generosity can open our lives to the very best God has to offer. In fact, the very best that God has to offer is exactly where we need to start.

## A Tradition Worth Keeping

Several years ago I read of the old Quaker tradition of keeping a gratitude journal. I was inspired by the idea, so I purchased a book with blank pages and titled it *My Ode to Joy.* Each morning I wrote a little thank-you note to God. I found it to be a way to start my day on a positive note. Little did I understand then how the discipline of writing down five things for which I am thankful every day would forever change my life.

When I first started, I found it easy to hit the big things—good parents, a wonderful husband, my children (and later my grandchildren), and, of course, a writing career I love. These precious gifts still make their way on to my list over and over. Today, when I reread journals from past years I see that as the months, then years trickled by, I began to dig deeper for things to add to my list. As I matured in my understanding of how God works, it wasn't only the good things, the pleasant, "happy" gifts for which I expressed appreciation. I began to see more clearly how God was using life's trials in unexpected ways for my good, so I began to write down my gratitude for the seemingly negative things in my life—my troubles, pains, and losses. With that knowledge I became more confident that God would see me through everything, and my gratitude grew deeper. In fact, the greatest example of giving thanks for negative things can be found in Corrie ten Boom's book *The Hiding Place.*[1]

## Fleas, God's Secret Weapon

During World War II, Corrie and her sister Betsie had been arrested in Holland for trying to help Jews escape the Holocaust. They ended up in Ravensbrück, one of the most infamous Nazi concentration camps. Their barracks had been built to hold 400 prisoners, but by the time the sisters arrived at the camp, the one-room building held more than 1,400 women.

Living conditions were insufferable. The women were housed like stacked cordwood on dirty, flea-infested straw that was strewn on wooden platforms. The fleas feasted night and day until everyone was covered in itchy, raised welts.

If it hadn't been for their Bible and the comfort the sisters were able to take from Betsie's readings, Corrie didn't know how they could have survived from day to day. If the guards had ventured into the room they would have discovered the forbidden Bible. Not only would it have been confiscated, but the consequences would have been brutal. Over and over, the two sisters wondered over the mystery of why the guards never inspected their barracks.

One morning Betsie read the Bible verse in 1 Thessalonians 5:18 that said, "Give thanks in all circumstances." She insisted that they put this into practice, feeling certain that giving thanks was the answer to their suffering. As Corrie tells the story, her sister named a litany of things they needed to thank God for—from the amazing circumstance that enabled the sisters to stay together, to the Bible she held in her hands, to the other women in the camp. But when Betsie began to thank God for the suffocating room and finally for the fleas, Corrie balked. It seemed impossible to Corrie to find anything for which to thank God in the deprivation of a concentration camp.

But Betsie insisted, reminding Corrie that God said, "In all circumstances." Corrie recalled standing in that room with all the other women, thanking God for the fleas and being certain that, for once, Betsie was wrong. Yet that prayer proved to be a turning point for the women. Their circumstances hadn't changed, but their attitude did. Betsie and Corrie began to connect with the women in a way that changed those barracks and the women imprisoned there. It wasn't until much later that Corrie discovered the reason the dreaded inspection never happened and their beloved Bible remained undiscovered. It was the very same reason she and Betsie were never stopped from having their much-anticipated Bible studies.

The fleas!

The guards refused to set foot into those barracks because of the out-of-control flea infestation. When Betsie took God at His word and thanked Him in all circumstances, she had no idea those fleas were actually a gift from God.

It's easy to be grateful for the sunshine, the good things, plenty of food, meeting the budget, and compliant children. But God tells us to express gratitude in *all* circumstances.

Think about it. That means we are called to offer thanks when the wind blows into our lives at hurricane force. We are asked to thank Him when the money runs out long before the end of the month and when the kids are pushing the boundaries and challenging us at every turn. It doesn't make any logical sense, does it?

Corrie ten Boom discovered the "sense" of giving thanks in all circumstances. She discovered the vital link between gratitude and *trust*. Through reading *The Hiding Place* and through the practice of keeping my own gratitude journal, I, too, have discovered this link. Though we may not understand the *whys* of our circumstances, by thanking God we grow to acknowledge that He is in control—that He can be trusted. We learn to release our iron-tight grip on our circumstances, and we experience a much-welcome reprieve from worry.

The importance of giving thanks is made clear in Philippians 4:6: "Do not be anxious about anything, but in everything, by prayer and petition, with thanksgiving, present your requests to God." Interesting, isn't it? The antidote for anxiety is to pray *with thanksgiving.*

## *Discovery*

*The act of gratitude reminds us that God is worthy of our trust.*

## Footsteps Worth Following

I admit learning to praise God in all circumstances takes practice. I find I need to be intentional and deliberate in doing so and make it a day-by-day, even minute-by-minute exercise. My grandparents, Anna and Anton Adler, were immigrants of German-Russian extraction who settled in the Dakotas. They were dirt farmers during the Great Depression of the 1930s. My grandparents rose long before dawn, greeting each day with anticipation. My grandfather labored in his fields only to see his crops fail year after year. When all seemed lost, he didn't give up. He looked toward the future. He heard of work picking fruit in the Yakima Valley in Washington State. Selling everything they had, my grandparents headed west with six children, leaving their two adult children behind, with their few remaining earthly possessions strapped to the back of their Model T Ford. They headed west, and without a backward glance, my grandfather left the farm behind. By all outward appearances he had failed just as the land had failed, and yet, as told in our family stories, my grandparents chose to thank God for the work ahead of them, rather than complain about what they had lost.

In the footsteps of my grandparents I, too, want to look at life with a sense of gratitude. I see my journal writing as starting my morning out on the positive note of practicing gratitude. Instead of grumbling over the drizzle outside my kitchen window, I can smile and remember that it's the rain that makes everything so green and lush in the Pacific Northwest.

I once read that there are more verses in the Bible that praise God than anything else. I'm not a Bible scholar, so I can't say for sure if that's true or not, but I do know that when we have a thankful heart, despite our circumstances, we lighten our load. Nothing jump-starts our gratitude like practicing the habit of praise. King David, who poured out his gratitude in verse after verse of the book of Psalms, was called a man after God's own heart. Isn't that what we'd like to be? Simply reading his psalms of praise is an ideal way to build gratitude into our lives.

## Checkout Lane Surprise

A few months ago I was in line at the supermarket. My cart was piled high and I was anxious to be on my way. I was grateful that the young woman in front of me only had a partially filled cart. As I watched her carefully unload her groceries, I could see that she seemed anxious. As the checker finished ringing up the groceries, the young woman leaned across the check stand, whispered something to the checker, and left—without her groceries. The checker piled the bags onto the cart and set it off to the side.

I guessed the scenario. The young woman didn't have enough money to pay for her purchase.

The clerk looked up at me and smiled, "Thanks for waiting. She had to go to the bank for more money."

I looked at the mountain of groceries in my cart, remembering my own scary days back in the early 1980s when I first decided I wanted to be a writer. My husband, Wayne, and I had four young children, and as a construction electrician, Wayne was often between jobs. I remembered well when we were feeding our young family of six on Wayne's unemployment check of $150 a week.

I felt that inner discomfort that I sometimes get when God nudges me to do something. I call these moments "divine appointments." It wasn't by accident that I turned up behind this young woman.

"How much were her groceries?" I asked.

The clerk looked up as if she hadn't understood my question.

"How much was the bill?" I repeated. She pulled the tape from the bag and told me. Then she shrugged her shoulders as if she didn't know why I'd be asking.

"Kindly add that amount to my bill," I told her.

The clerk stopped checking my groceries. I was glad my piled-high cart had kept others from lining up behind me.

"She may not even come back," the woman cautioned. "Sometimes if a person doesn't have enough money she says she'll come back because she's embarrassed. She probably won't return, so save your money."

"No," I insisted, "I want to pay for her groceries."

"She probably won't be back," she said in a flippant tone. "What do you want me to do with them then?"

"Give the food to someone in need," I suggested.

I could see the clerk had never had someone offer to pay for someone else's groceries. She appeared shocked and continued to stare at me. "Why are you doing this?" she asked.

I explained that at one time I'd been in that young woman's situation. I remembered wondering how I'd feed my family. I told her how grateful I was for all that God had given me. I tried to explain that with gratitude comes the urge to share.

She didn't say a word, and I was left wondering if I was babbling on far too long. What I was doing didn't make a lot of sense. The clerk was right—the woman who'd left might very well not return. Yet I couldn't shake the feeling that God wanted me to do this. I've come to recognize those promptings from God and learned not to resist them.

Slowly the clerk returned to ringing up my groceries. "I want to know more about God," she said simply.

That's when it hit me. This nudge from God wasn't about the young woman who left her groceries behind. God hadn't nudged me for her sake, but for the clerk's sake! For whatever reason, she needed to witness an act of generosity done in the Lord's name.

I thought of Corrie ten Boom's fleas. In this case, my own gift of generosity was having a benefit I had never imagined, just as the fleas had a benefit Corrie had never imagined. I thought I was helping the young woman needing groceries, but the Lord had set His sights on the clerk. Something my Florida pastor, James E. Biles Sr., once said in a sermon came to mind. I remembered being so struck by his words that I wrote them down on the margin of my bulletin: "We aren't only called to share the gospel. We are called to *show* the gospel."

Look at it this way: had God not been tutoring me in the habit of gratitude, I might have been stewing about the delay caused by the young woman's inability to pay. Instead I was able to listen to that still, small voice that sometimes gently urges me to act. Had I rationalized that the young woman might never come back for her groceries, I might have missed blessing the person God intended. Although I frequently shopped at that store I never saw her again, and yet I feel God planted her in my path that day for His purposes.

Keep the eyes of your heart open for those God may want to help through you today.

## *Discovery*

*Practicing an attitude of gratitude spills over to acts of generosity.*

## The Science of Gratitude

My own discovery about the importance of gratitude was largely developed as I read the Bible. But did you know that science confirms the importance of gratitude as well?

Two researchers, R. A. Emmons of the University of California, Davis, and M. E. McCullough of the University of Miami, have been researching the dimensions and perspectives of gratitude. Their findings fascinate me and have been the basis of dozens of articles in scientific journals and bulletins. Take a look with me at what they learned.

Their experiments demonstrated that those who kept gratitude journals on a weekly basis exercised more regularly, reported fewer illness symptoms, felt better about their lives as a whole, and were more optimistic about the upcoming week compared to those who recorded troubles or neutral life events. As they continued to experiment, they found that participants who kept gratitude lists were more likely to have made progress over a two-month period toward their most important personal goals—academic, interpersonal, and health based—compared to the subjects in their control group.[2] So gratitude not only contributed to better overall health but helped people reach important goals. Think about it. Our Creator designed us to benefit when we give thanks.

And that's not all. Here's something else the researchers discovered: a daily gratitude exercise where young adults regularly focused on specific things for which they were thankful resulted in higher reported levels of the positive states of alertness, enthusiasm, determination, attentiveness, and energy.

Remember that I said that generosity grows out of gratitude? The study also showed that participants in the daily gratitude experiment were more likely to report having helped someone with a personal problem or having offered emotional support to another. You see, when gratitude becomes a habit, then generosity seems to follow naturally.

In a sample of adults with neuromuscular disease, a twenty-one-day gratitude intervention resulted in greater amounts of energy, positive moods, a greater sense of feeling connected to others, more optimistic ratings of one's life, and better sleep duration and quality relative to a control group.

Wow!

But there's more. Stephen Post, PhD, professor of bioethics at Case Western Reserve University's School of Medicine, is the author of *Why Good Things Happen to Good People.* In an article in *Guideposts,* "The Power of Gratitude," he shares five things he discovered about gratitude:

**1.** *Gratitude defends.* Just fifteen minutes a day focusing on the things you're grateful for will significantly increase your body's natural antibodies.

**2.** *Gratitude sharpens.* Naturally grateful people are more focused mentally and are measurably less vulnerable to clinical depression.

**3.** *Gratitude calms.* A grateful state of mind induces a physiological state called resonance that's associated with healthier blood pressure and heart rate.

**4.** *Gratitude strengthens.* Caring for others is draining. But grateful caregivers are healthier and more capable than less grateful ones.

**5.** *Gratitude heals.* Recipients of donated organs who have the most grateful attitudes heal faster.[3]

## *Discovery*

*Gratitude gives back. When we practice gratitude, not only do we grow in our trust of God, but we benefit physically, emotionally, and spiritually.*

## Gratitude as a Prerequisite to Giving

As we acknowledge all we have, as we learn to praise God for all He has done for us, God helps us pry our fingers off our possessions, our BlackBerrys, and our bank statements. This brings us full circle. Can you see why we explored gratitude before we set off on our journey to discover the power of generosity? Gratitude is the basis for giving. Grumpy, stingy people cannot live in the spirit of generosity. In order to be able to open our hands to give, we first have to give thanks for all we've been given. It's just that simple!

## ♦ SIMPLE ACTS OF GRATITUDE ♦

❖ Begin a gratitude journal. Each day write five things for which you are grateful.

❖ Practice praise. Nothing opens our eyes to the gifts we have been given more than focusing on the Giver. Find at least one new thing to praise God for each day.

❖ Stay alert for those "God nudges" and be grateful when you sense them. When you feel like you should be doing something for someone, act on it. Keep track of those nudges. Write them down, noting how you responded and the outcome. When we practice listening for that still small voice we become better at hearing it.

❖ Thank God in all circumstances. This means that sometimes you'll thank Him for the "fleas" in your life.

**Do not forget to do good and**

**to share with others,**

**for with such sacrifices God is pleased.**

*Hebrews 13:16*

# Two

## Loaves, Fishes, and Miracle Math

### The Mystery of Sharing

From the time I was a little girl, we always bowed our heads at the dinner table to ask God to bless our food. "Bless us, O Lord, for these thy gifts which we are about to receive from Thy bounty, through Christ our Lord. Amen."

Having come from good, solid farm stock, I've always known that food comes to our table only by the grace of God, but I never gave much thought to the act of saying grace. To me it was just a simple act of gratitude. I never thought about the times Jesus blessed the bread before breaking it. And I never pondered what the act meant.

We have explored how gratitude connects to generosity, but before we go much further, let me do what I do best, and that's telling a story. This is one I've loved from the time I was a little girl. It comes from the Bible. If you'd like to read it yourself you can find it in four different places: Matthew 14:13–21; Mark 6:32–44; Luke 9:10–17; and John 6:1–13. This might well be one of the most important of all the miracles mentioned in the Bible. I'll tell you why.

When God wants us to pay close attention, He repeats the message. In this case He did it four times. Other than the Resurrection, it's the only miracle in the Bible repeated in each of the Gospels.

Picture a young boy, living near the Sea of Galilee in the first century A.D.

"Mother," he said as he came into the yard where she knelt. His mother didn't stop what she was doing. She took a wooden paddle and slid it into the clay oven, scooting it around until she worked it under all the small mounds of baked bread. The boy breathed deeply, inhaling the scent of barley as she removed the loaves, setting them on top of the oven.

She looked up at him and smiled, squinting into the sun.

"Father is going to find Jesus and listen to him teach. Can I go with him?" He tried to stand straight so he'd look big enough to hold his own in the huge crowds that had begun to follow Jesus of Nazareth.

His father came out of the doorway of their home, pulling a cloak over his shoulder. "I should be back before nightfall," he said.

His mother took a cloth and wrapped five tiny rough barley loaves and two small dried fish. "Take these just in case you get hungry." Her son was happy to oblige.

It didn't take long for the father and son to find the huge crowd that followed the Teacher. They watched and listened for most of the morning. When Jesus finished speaking, He got into a boat with the men who traveled with Him.

"Come, son, let's go home."

"Look, Father." The boy shaded his eyes with his hand. "The Teacher's boat is stalled by a headwind."

The crowds began hurrying along the shore. "Jesus and His disciples are heading toward Bethsaida," one man yelled. "If we hurry, we can meet them on the shore as they land."

The boy and his father joined the running, stumbling crowd. His stomach growled with hunger as he ran to keep up. He'd been so engrossed in the words of Jesus all morning that he hadn't remembered to eat. He tugged on the satchel tied to his belt to make sure his lunch was still secure. If he asked Father to stop so they could eat, he knew they might miss some of the Teacher's words. He could wait.

The crowd reached the opposite shore just as the Teacher and His men arrived.

The boy looked at Jesus. He looked tired. His followers stepped forward as if they were going to tell the crowd to leave, but Jesus put his palm out toward them, motioning them to stop. He moved toward the crowd and once again began to heal and teach.

The boy didn't remember his hunger until late in the day when the Teacher's followers came through the crowds.

"Does anyone have any food?" asked one. "The Master says the people are hungry and we need to feed them."

No one else had any food, and the boy said nothing.

"There are about five thousand men here," said one of the disciples to another, "and that doesn't even count the women and children."

Another of the Teacher's men shook his head and said, "I've figured it would take a full eight months' wages to buy enough food to feed this crowd."

They asked again, "Does anyone have any food?"

The boy thought about the lunch his mother had given him. He was hungry, and if he gave it away, there would be nothing for him. His looked to his father and knew that he was thinking the same thing. Yet, the words of the Teacher had touched his heart. It was within his means to give something back for all that the Teacher had given him.

"I have a lunch," the boy volunteered in a small voice. He held out the scrap of cloth with his small loaves and fishes.

"Son, are you sure you want to do this?" his father asked. "You must be hungry too and there's only a little food here, just enough for the two of us."

"If the Teacher needs my lunch, then I want to give it."

The disciple accepted the lunch, putting a hand on the boy's shoulder. "Thank you. I don't know what good it will do with a crowd like this, but Jesus said to collect any food."

The boy's stomach growled again as the men went toward the Teacher with his lunch. He was proud that he could share what he had with Jesus.

Soon afterward Jesus asked the crowd to divide into groups of about fifty men and to sit on the tall spring grass. The boy watched as his father helped count their group off. Everyone sat down, waiting to see what Jesus had in mind. The boy sat on the very edge so he could see what the Teacher would do with his lunch.

Jesus took it and raised it in His hands, thanking God for it.

The boy didn't mind that Jesus thanked God for the lunch. He knew that all things came from the heavenly Father. When Jesus finished praying, He seemed to look right at the boy.

He broke the tiny loaves into a basket. The boy blinked and then rubbed his eyes. Where did all that bread come from? Was it a trick? No, that was his mother's rough barley bread. He'd eaten it every day of his life.

The Teacher's men kept bringing one basket after another, and

Jesus broke the loaves and filled the baskets. The same thing happened to the fish.

It didn't make any sense, but it tasted as good as if his mother had taken the bread right out of the oven. He ate as much as his stomach could hold—much more than the five loaves and two fishes. Looking around, he could see that everyone had eaten his fill. Amazing!

The disciples came around with baskets to collect all of the leftovers. Leftovers? How could there be leftovers?

The boy knew he had witnessed a miracle unlike any other he had ever seen.

## All It Takes Is One Simple Act

The boy in our story had nothing more than a skimpy lunch and the willingness to give it to Jesus. The Lord took that lunch and asked His Father to bless it. That tiny lunch, after it had been blessed, fed five thousand men and probably a similar number of women and children.

In this book I'll be talking about generously sharing our resources, our time, our words, our acts of hospitality—things that all too often seem in short supply—and what happens once we do. All the child had were a few sardines and stone-sized loaves of bread. The real gift was his willingness to offer it. Like the little boy, we need not be ashamed of bringing our small lunch to Jesus. When we think of generosity, we too often think of grand gestures and sweeping acts of charity. But when Jesus gave us an example, He focused on just one simple act.

### Discovery

*If we are willing to hold our resources with an open hand,
there's no telling what God can do.*

## God Multiplies Our Giving

That small lunch—or our meager resources—can feed thousands when Jesus blesses it. That's where something truly wonderful happens. You've heard yourself moan, "I've only got twenty-four hours in a day." So why is it when you start giving some of that time away, it feels as if you've found extra hours? Why is it when a financially strapped young couple decide to adopt a World Vision child, they don't miss the money? It makes no sense economically or scientifically, but it happens over and over. You'll hear people talk about how frazzled they were timewise—running in a hundred different directions—but when they began to volunteer at the homeless shelter things began to fall into place.

It's the magic of multiplication. This is what happens when we are willing to bring our gifts to God.

### Discovery

*The real miracle is the multiplication of limited resources.
It may not compute on your accountant's calculator, but it's a
central element in God's economy.*

## We Can't Outgive God

I know you've heard this cliché—we can't outgive God—but there's deep truth in the familiar words. The boy got back his lunch plus much, much more. That tells us who God is. He asks that we give, but when we do, He showers us with blessings. "Give, and it will be given to you. A good measure, pressed down, shaken together and running over, will be poured into your lap. For with the measure you use, it will be measured to you" (Luke 6:38).

Trust me, this book will not be another book touting a get-rich-quick scheme or the idea that if you do things right, God will make you wealthy beyond your wildest dreams. The kind of giving God talks about is much more complex than "if you give a dollar, God will return it multiplied," although that may sometimes happen.

## *Discovery*

*Here's where the real power of generosity comes in.
Often, the more we give, the more we receive.*

## There's Enough to Cover the Need

After a meal, my friend's aunt used to place her silverware on the edge of her plate, fold her napkin, and declare that she'd had an "elegant sufficiency." "Sufficient" is a powerful word, especially in a hungry world. With God's multiplication as part of the equation, we can expect miracles. Together, we have enough to cover the need, but like the boy, we must be willing to offer our own fishes and loaves for the miracle to take place.

## *Discovery*

*God multiplies our giving. In His hands each act of generosity we offer Him, no matter how small, becomes part of this miracle of multiplication.*

*Encourage one another and*

*build each other up,*

*just as in fact you are doing.*

*1 Thessalonians 5:11*

# Three

## Keys, Candy, and Army Men

### *The Act of Encouragement*

I was a little girl who craved encouragement.

To say I struggled in school is putting it mildly. I'm dyslexic, but in those days, the teachers didn't have a name for this particular learning disability. All I knew is that I couldn't read the way the other kids in my class did. Everything seemed to come easy for them, but not for me. My problems with reading showed up early. In first grade I was placed in the Robin reading group at school; the only girl in the "slow" group.

Even at that young age, I was confused as to why I struggled when I loved books and words so much. My mother told me that the first time I was given a book, I grabbed hold of it with both hands and pressed it against my heart. Fortunately I was intelligent enough to learn how to sight-read so the teachers passed me from one grade to the next without realizing I didn't understand the basic reading concepts. In fact I was ten years old and in the fifth grade before I learned how to sound out words.

In my third-grade parent/teacher conference, I sat with my mother. As I looked around the room at all our best papers pinned to the walls, I longed to hear a word of encouragement. I loved school. It was difficult, but I worked hard. I'll never forget what my teacher said. She put a hand on my shoulder and said, "Mrs. Adler, Debbie is a nice little girl and I enjoy having her in my class, but she'll never do well in school."

Never.

Those words became part of my life story, and do you know what? She was right. I never excelled in school. Now that I've been a mom and a grandmother, I wonder if those words were a self-fulfilling prophecy. What if she had spoken different words, like, "Debbie tries so hard, I'm guessing it will be just a matter of time until academics click for her." Would I have clung to those words, taking hope from them? Would I have tried to find a way to unlock my learning disability earlier?

That little girl who hungered for encouragement is still tucked inside me. She's helped me realize that there's a child in all of us who craves a word of encouragement.

We are so unaware of how simple comments can change people's lives. My friend Linda Miller recalls how a few words of encouragement in junior high school altered her life dramatically. On her last day before graduating from junior high school one of her teachers stopped her in the hall and said, "Linda, you are much smarter than you think. If you want to, you can be the valedictorian of your high school class." Linda never thought of herself as especially smart, but that teacher planted a seed of hopeful expectation in her mind. And four years later when Linda graduated, she was valedictorian of her high school class.

## The Key That Opens Locked Doors

Every one of us has potential stored inside just waiting to be developed. We are filled with promise and possibility. But for many of us, that potential is locked away behind a closed door. Our doors may be made of disappointment, failure, embarrassment, or lack of confidence. Maybe we were teased or belittled. Or maybe it simply never occurred to us that we could try something new and succeed; we were simply never exposed to a particular opportunity.

Each person in your life has such doors. And you hold the key to unlocking some of those doors with your words of encouragement. Maybe God is ready to use you to unleash their creativity, stir their passions, embolden them to stretch beyond their past experience, and strengthen them to face their challenges.

Take a look at the invitation God has given us to be generous with words of encouragement. "Therefore encourage one another and build each other up, just as in fact you are doing" (1 Thessalonians 5:11). When we offer plentiful gifts of honest encouragement we have the privilege of taking part in the creation of—the building up of—the special people in our lives. Talk about an opportunity to have a lasting influence!

My friend told me about a young couple she knows. By all accounts, Jennifer is brilliant. Growing up, she excelled in ballet, choreographed for a liturgical dance troupe, created beautiful textile pieces, and was a natural leader at school and church. Her class voted her homecoming queen. She was valedictorian of her large urban high school and she was accepted to UC Berkeley, where she graduated with honors. Jennifer was accepted at a top physical therapy school and landed the finest internship available. She had her PhD before she was out of her twenties.

When Jennifer met the man she would marry, several of her friends had reservations. It was clear that Garth loved her and they enjoyed many of the same things—foreign films, good cooking, and urban living, among others. But Garth had barely managed to get through high school. He was classified a "resource" student during all his school years, though most of us are more familiar with the more common term, "special education." Garth spent many of his school years refusing to acknowledge the insulting names like "retard." When Jennifer met him, he had an excellent job with one of the utility companies and had already risen to supervisor. His manager urged Garth to get his degree. Because Garth is so personable, the manager knew that if Garth had the requisite degree, the sky would be the limit for him careerwise.

It didn't seem possible that a brilliant, well-rounded person with a PhD and a special ed student could build a life together. Jennifer believed so. She knew what a fine man Garth was. She also knew that she'd had a struggle in school herself. It wasn't until third grade that she began to read, and she knew it was her parents' encouragement and involvement that made the difference. When she and Garth began to talk about building a life together, she encouraged him to give college a try. He nervously agreed. Garth's special ed grades had been good, so his high school transcripts looked good on paper. He was accepted into a fine private college.

That's when the work began. He and Jennifer experimented with learning styles. They discovered that he was an auditory learner—he learned primarily through hearing. They began by having Jennifer read his texts to him.

In the early semesters, she made old-fashioned flash cards to help him study for tests. He wrote well but needed help with organization and spelling. That first year he and Jennifer spent most of their free time studying together. Sometimes her mom and dad helped in the same way they helped her during her early school years.

By the second year, it began to click. Garth caught the rhythm and did more on his own. By the time he was an upperclassman he'd pretty much figured it out.

When Garth graduated from his prestigious school with honors, he knew it was Jennifer's encouragement and belief in him that had unlocked his fears and made it possible for him to get his degree. His graduation party took place just a couple of months after their wedding.

*Discovery*

*Sometimes all it takes is one simple act of believing in someone to unlock his or her potential.*

## The Difference Between Praise and Encouragement

A battle over praise versus encouragement has been raging in educational circles for a long while now. We've always thought it important to praise the things children do. How many times do you overhear parents saying "good job" to their children?

According to many psychologists, in the rush to build self-esteem, many parents and teachers overpraise. Children begin to expect praise for every little task and feel unappreciated if they don't receive effusive words. They become praise junkies.

A friend tells the story of trying to potty-train her little girl, Mandy. She put a bottle of nonpareils—the tiny candies used to decorate cakes—on the counter beside the toilet. Every time Mandy was successful she got a tiny candy reward. With a sparkle in her eye, Mandy would stick her little hand out making a motioning movement with her fingers, and she'd say, "Canny, Mommy." She loved that candy so much, guess what this bright little girl learned to do? She learned how to control her bladder so that she could go every few minutes to get the maximum "canny." Her mom learned that rewards—praise—often lead to unintended consequences.

I know a small-business owner who tells me that she sees far too many overpraised young adults who can barely begin a task without needing the "canny" of praise. It cripples them. They are motivated to perform for the praise of others instead of learning self-satisfaction with a job well done.

One definition of praise is "to voice approbation, commendation, or esteem." All of those words have judgment built in. The person giving the praise deems you worthy of commendation, like the words "good job." We're evaluating and giving our thumbs-up.

Encouragement, on the other hand, looks to the effort behind a job. Instead of hearing, "That's the best cake you've ever made," encouragement might be something like, "I think it's wonderful that when you have free time you choose to bake for your family." Praise too often refers to the product, while encouragement focuses on the act itself and the heart behind the action.

Had my third-grade teacher been in the habit of encouraging, she might have said to my mother, "I've noticed that Debbie never seems to give up, no matter how hard the task."

I love how the Apostle Paul wrote of this when he charged us with the task of encouragement in 1 Thessalonians 5:14–15: "And we urge you, brothers, warn those who are idle, encourage the timid, help the weak, be patient with everyone. Make sure that nobody pays back wrong for wrong, but always try to be kind to each other and to everyone else." Good words.

So if we're called to give encouragement, we need to begin to exercise our encouragement muscles. I remember a song Gloria Gaither wrote for children called "I Am a Promise." In that song a chorus of children's voices sang, "I am a promise, I am a possibility." Bingo! That's what we all are in God's eyes. Are you ready to see the promise in the people God brings into your life? Are you ready to look for ways to unlock their doors?

## *Discovery*

*The act of encouragement begins in seeing people as God sees them,*
*for all they can be, for who they are becoming.*

## An Encouraging Word

My grandson, Cameron, is not an outdoors boy. No matter how much my daughter, Jennifer, tries to encourage outdoor play, he'd rather stay indoors doing quiet things. One summer day, though, he just got it in his head that he knew how to arrange army men for battle. This happened during the Iraq War. The news had obviously affected my sensitive, tender-hearted Cameron. He spent the entire day outside creating intricate formations of little green army men.

When he'd finished, Cameron insisted his mother take a picture of it in case she happened to run into an army officer. That way Cameron could share his battle plan so the officer would know how to fight the war. Jennifer, who knew not a single military strategist, just smiled and got out her camera, dutifully taking pictures of his work.

Well it just so happened that Jennifer came to New York with me for Ruth Stafford Peale's one hundredth birthday party. The party was a glittering affair, and I visited with many people I'd known through the Guideposts Foundation, including Dr. June Scobee Rodgers. June's first husband, Dick Scobee, was commander of the space shuttle *Challenger*, which tragically exploded seventy-three seconds after takeoff. As we visited, June introduced us to her second husband, Don Rodgers, who is a retired three-star general. Jennifer looked at me and laughed. What were the chances of her meeting a military strategist at a birthday party? She took out one of the photos Cameron had insisted she take and she gave it to General Rodgers, explaining what Cameron had done.

The general looked it over and later took the time to write Cameron a letter. In it he said, "Cameron, your mom shared with me your battle formation plans. I've looked it over and studied it and I want you to know that I can see your line of thought. And with your permission I will share this with my friends at the Pentagon." I can't begin to tell you what that did to that little boy's self-esteem. It built him up in a way that nothing else could have ever done. And it came at a time when Cameron badly needed encouragement.

When we talk about the power of generosity, I think the picture of a three-star general penning a letter to an eight-year-old boy, generously offering words of encouragement for his efforts, is a perfect example.

### Encouragement as the Antidote to Failure

I know how important encouragement is.

Twenty-five years ago, there was nothing I wanted more in the world than to become a published writer. I've told this story often, but it is so much a part of who I am, I need to repeat it. I had struggled for years, trying to stay at home to write and raise our children when what we desperately needed was for me to go out and find a paying job. Wayne worked two jobs so I could do that, working as an electrician days and teaching apprenticeship classes at night.

I had finally sold an anecdote to a magazine. When I heard that there would be a writer's conference nearby and that two New York editors would be there, I took some of those precious dollars I had earned and registered. Writers were allowed to submit their manuscripts in advance. Ten of those manuscripts would be reviewed by the editors. New York editors!

When I was notified that my manuscript had been chosen as one of those ten to be reviewed, I could hardly contain my excitement. I told Wayne, "I just know I'm going to be successful. I'm really going to make it."

When one of the editors walked up to the lectern to begin the critique of the manuscripts, the first thing she said was, "Out of the ten manuscripts we reviewed, only one showed real promise."

It took everything I had not to jump up out of my seat and say, "That would be mine."

It wasn't. When the time came for her to talk about my manuscript she had the audience laughing over what she called the implausibility of my plot. She ripped the story to shreds. I was numb.

I've always been determined, however, so after the presentation, I went up to the editor and introduced myself. I told her I would revise, rewrite, do whatever it took to make the manuscript publishable.

I will never forget the look in her eyes as she leaned forward, pressed her hand on my arm, and said, "Honey, throw that manuscript away."

Throw it away. I will never forget those words. Were it not for the never-flagging encouragement of my family, I might have taken that critique to heart and not only thrown that manuscript away but thrown my dream away as well.

My story has a happy ending. It wasn't long after that I sold my very first book. Know what book it was? That same book I was told to throw away.

I love what Stephen King wrote in his book *On Writing*: "My wife made a crucial difference . . . If she had suggested that the time I spent writing stories . . . in the laundry room of our rented trailer . . . was wasted time, I think a lot of the heart would have gone out of me . . . Whenever I see a first novel dedicated to a wife (or a husband), I smile and think, *There's someone who knows*. Writing is a lonely job. Having someone who believes in you makes a lot of difference. They don't have to make speeches. Just believing is usually enough."[1]

I laughed when I heard a writer introduce her husband at a writing conference as her "patron of the arts." Anyone who's followed a dream to write knows that the financial rewards are few and far between, especially in the early years. A spouse who helps support the writer offers far more than words of encouragement.

I wish I could credit the anonymous person who compiled this list of "failures," but I think it's encouraging to share with anyone feeling frustrated by a lack of success:

~ Einstein was four years old before he could speak.

~ Isaac Newton did poorly in grade school and was considered "unpromising."

~ When Thomas Edison was a youngster, his teacher told him he was too stupid to learn anything. He was counseled to go into a field where he might succeed by virtue of his pleasant personality.

~ F. W. Woolworth got a job in a dry goods store when he was twenty-one, but his boss would not permit him to wait on customers because he "didn't have enough sense to close a sale."

~ Michael Jordan was cut from his high school basketball team.

~ A newspaper editor fired Walt Disney because he "lacked imagination and had no original ideas."

~ Winston Churchill failed the sixth grade and had to repeat it because he did not complete the tests that were required for promotion.

~ Babe Ruth struck out 1,330 times, a major league record.

## Encouragement Changes the Encourager

There's another interesting thing that happens when we cultivate the habit of encouragement. Offering encouragement changes the encourager. The more we look to find ways to encourage others, the more we'll find ourselves being encouraged. We have scientific data and studies proving this to be true. We understand that, like the loaves and fishes, it's simply the miracle of multiplication. Let me say it again: *The more we encourage, the more we are encouraged ourselves.*

As Mother Teresa of Calcutta once said, "Our life of poverty is as necessary as the work itself. Only in heaven will we see how much we owe to the poor for helping us to love God better because of them."

Jean Nidetch weighed more than 200 pounds in the early sixties, when out of desperation she went to the New York City De-

partment of Health to get a diet. She worked hard to follow it
but became discouraged by how far she had to go. She knew she
needed encouragement, so she invited six overweight friends to
her Queens, New York, home to encourage each other.

Today, almost fifty years later, Weight Watchers, the program
that grew out of that need to encourage others, has taught millions of members how to lose weight and live healthier lives. In any
given week members attend one of over 44,000 Weight Watchers
meetings in thirty countries worldwide. Why was it so important
for Nidetch to encourage people take control of their lives? To
answer that, she tells a story. When she was a teenager, she used
to cross a park where she saw mothers sitting around visiting while
the toddlers sat on their swings, with no one to push them. "I'd give
them a push," says Nidetch. "And you know what happens when
you push a kid on a swing? Pretty soon he's pumping, doing it himself. That's what my role in life is—I'm there to give others a push."

The interesting thing is that when Jean Nidetch began encouraging others, she herself was encouraged. Who could have imagined that discouraged, overweight housewife starting a worldwide
movement?

One simple act of encouragement can be the key that unlocks
those long-buried treasures or never-dreamed-of possibilities. Encouragement might take the form of a simple word of affirmation.
It might be telling someone you believe she can succeed. It might
even be a letter from a three-star general. As we cultivate the habit
of encouragement, we discover the power of encouraging others.
Not only will we be turning a key that unlocks their potential, but
we will be living up to our own potential to build up another person.

## ◢IMPLE ◢CTS OF ◢NCOURAGEMENT

✦ Discover your own comfort zone when it comes to encouragement. Are you most comfortable with giving quick little words of encouragement? Are you best at putting things in writing? Do you prefer to pick up the phone? Would you rather meet face-to-face to encourage a friend? Or are you a whiz at text-messaging little snippets of encouragement?

✦ Once you've discovered how you best like to encourage, set a goal. Maybe you'll try to phone someone every week with an encouraging word. Perhaps you'll e-mail your children every day with a little bit of fun and encouragement. Or would you rather write a long, meaningful letter after spending time praying for your friend? Whatever feels right, set a goal and follow through.

✦ Keep an encouragement journal. Write down the ways and days you offered encouragement, along with any responses or outcomes. In a separate section you may want to note the bits of encouragement that came back to you. It will be interesting to see which section fills up faster. Remember what I said earlier? You can't outgive God.

Let your light shine before men,

that they may see your good deeds

and praise your Father in heaven.

*Matthew 5:16*

## Four

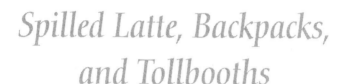

# Spilled Latte, Backpacks, and Tollbooths

## *The Habit of Good Deeds*

After a long trip on the East Coast, I was heading back to Seattle. I had gotten up at three in the morning to catch a car to Newark Airport. As I arrived at my gate, I noticed that the Starbucks had just opened. Right away a long line formed as caffeine-starved travelers sought relief. I patiently waited my turn and was rewarded with my favorite vanilla fat-free latte. I couldn't wait to get settled so I could take that first sip; the anticipation is always half the pleasure. Coffee at last. I juggled my purse, my knitting bag, and my carry-on into my chair. While I was putting everything down, wouldn't you know it, the latte slipped from my hand and tumbled onto the carpet. The entire latte spilled out. First of all, it was highly embarrassing as everyone at the gate stared in my direction, and second,

I wasn't about to stand in the line again because I'd been so incredibly clumsy. I wanted to kick myself for being so careless.

I didn't feel I could leave the mess, so I picked up a thick wad of napkins. The last thing I wanted was to bend over and expose my least favorite part of my anatomy to everybody. So I did the next best thing. I papered the carpet with napkins and did a little dance, stomping on the covered area in an attempt to blot up the latte. Of course, all eyes in the gate area watched my every move. And it wasn't just one gate area. There happened to be three gates, packed full, that all converged on this spot.

When I had soaked up the liquid as best I could, I picked up the cup and soppy napkins and put the whole mess in the garbage. I then sat down, trying to be invisible.

As I settled in and reached for my knitting, a businessman came by and said, "You know, I'm going to go get myself a cup of coffee. May I get you something?"

What a generous gesture. "That's so nice. Here let me pay you." I reached for my purse.

He shook his head, "No, this is my good deed for the day." And he went and got me a latte.

That simple act of kindness had a profound effect on me. I was amazed that somebody would be that kind. I felt good about it all day. Since that time I have made the effort to practice doing a good deed every single day. What I've learned is that these random acts of kindness don't necessarily have to be big to make a difference.

## Little Things

The other day I was at the grocery store. When I arrived, the lot was full and I had to park a long way away. After shopping and loading the groceries into the car, I noticed there wasn't a convenient area where I could return the shopping cart. Most of the carts were bumped up on planting islands or left in a parking space. As I looked for a place to stow it, I decided I'd just take it back. It would be my good deed so that nobody would risk running into the cart and it wouldn't take up an otherwise free parking space. It was just a small thing. But as I was getting close I saw a woman slowly and painfully get out of her car. She had obviously had some kind of surgery or suffered from a condition that made walking difficult. All the handicapped spaces had been taken, and the closest she could get was about four or five spaces back. There I was with my cart.

I said, "Here, let me give you this cart." She was so grateful because it made it much easier for her walk into the store. Now I would never have seen her or even thought about it if I hadn't been returning that cart—my tiny good deed. So just one simple act like that can have a ripple effect.

The outcome of that man's buying me a latte has been amazing. It opened my eyes to small possibilities. The other day I was in a grocery store line—I know it sounds like I spend a lot of time in the grocery, but remember, I'm a frequent eater and food is important to me—and there was a girl about ten years old behind me. She had two candy bars and I had a big cart of groceries. She was going to have to wait for me to get through the whole cart of groceries and pay for them, so I just said to the clerk, "Put her candy bars on my tab and give her a bag so she doesn't have to wait." That little girl just beamed. Her smile was worth far more than the dollar or so those two candy bars cost me.

## A Good Deed for Every Lifestyle

Doing regular acts of kindness is part of living in a spirit of generosity. Eventually the habit will slip seamlessly into your life. Think of ways to do things that fit with your lifestyle. For years I taught Sunday school class, but my traveling schedule doesn't make that possible any longer. I miss it. Unfortunately I'm not able to serve in the church in ways that I once did. So the things that I do are simple.

Being a natural-born storyteller, I volunteer to tell a story for the Awana group twice a year. I make up fun Bible quiz games for the different age groups and give the children small rewards if they answer the questions correctly. These young hearts are tender toward God and I receive far more than I give.

In recent months our church in Port Orchard started a backpack ministry. There are a growing number of hungry children in our community who go home and are without food on the weekends. The school provides breakfast and lunch for them Monday through Friday, but they don't have anything on the weekends. So our church bought backpacks to fill with food every week and send home with the children on Friday afternoon. I'm not there every week to work on the backpacks, so Wayne and I committed to help supply the food. Once a month we go to Costco and buy cans of tuna, dried fruit, pudding packs, raisins, and a multitude of other items the church uses to pack these backpacks. When the church started the Backpack Ministry, there were only ten children needing food. Now they are packing 150 backpacks every week. It's become emblematic of our church philosophy. We don't want to *attend* church. We want to *be* the church. We want to be like Jesus when He went out among the people. The question our pastor asks us is, "If this church were to close down tomorrow would anybody notice?" Now that's a good question.

I've noticed that once the habit of good deeds ignites, it spreads like a California wildfire. It's that magic of multiplication we talked about earlier. You do a simple good deed and before you know it, the acts of kindness have multiplied. In our church it's become contagious. Just last month a group of women came together and sewed fleece scarves to tuck into the backpacks so that the kids would have something warm for the winter.

When one person steps forward, it can lead to a chain reaction. As I'm writing this, there are a series of ads on television by an insurance company that show someone doing a small act of kindness for someone else. The next frame shows that person doing a good deed for another person. Two or three more frames continue the chain. This sequence makes for a satisfying ad, one based solidly in truth. When we do a good deed, it gets passed along.

### *Discovery*

*Good deeds are contagious.*

## Hit-and-Run Generosity

So, what kind of good deeds can you do? Further along we'll talk about service, which is usually more involved and often more time-consuming. Here we are talking about quick acts of kindness—a hit-and-run kind of generosity. I love what William Wordsworth had to say about it: "That best portion of a good man's life; / His little, nameless, unremembered acts / of kindness and love."

The key to doing good deeds is to make them simple and meaningful. For instance, a high school handed out one thousand greeting cards to their students and had them write a specific, meaningful note of thanks to someone at school. It was uncomplicated, only taking one thirty-minute study period. But the teachers, cafeteria workers, secretaries, janitors, and administrators who received the cards will treasure them forever. The lessons learned by the students, both in letter writing and expressing gratitude, are priceless.

A friend of mine and her husband buy gift cards from fast food restaurants. They keep them in the car. Every time they pass a homeless person or a panhandler, they roll down the window, greet him in the Lord's name, and hand him a card for a nearby restaurant. That way they know the person will get a warm meal and they don't run the risk of enabling substance abuse, in case that's a problem. It takes little more than planning ahead and setting aside a bit of money for the gift cards.

## Random Acts of Kindness

Did you know there's a foundation that exists for the purpose of encouraging good deeds? It's called the Random Acts of Kindness Foundation. On their Web site they have stories, ideas, and resources for joining the movement of those who want to do good deeds.

My friend experienced one of those good deeds. She was driving a friend to the San Francisco Airport. As she turned onto the approach to the San Mateo–Hayward Bridge, she saw the sign— BRIDGE TOLL $4.00. She says it wasn't until she automatically reached for her purse in the console that she remembered unzipping the bill compartment the night before and handing every last dollar to her husband to get pizza for dinner.

This friend prided herself on being a planner. She had never before forgotten to bring money on the two-hundred-mile round-trip into the city. As she rolled up to the tollbooth, she turned in embarrassment to ask her friend to borrow the money for the toll. Instead the attendant waved her through. "The car ahead of you paid your toll and said to tell you to have a happy day," he said.

They both burst out laughing. The quirky generosity of a stranger occurred on the only day my friend was ever caught penniless. She believes it was far too unusual to be mere coincidence. The bridge toll wasn't the real gift. The stranger's generosity reminded her that God even cares about the seemingly little glitches in our lives.

Since that time my friend says she has often paid for the car following hers.

After the familiar "A Time for Everything" passage in Ecclesiastes is the following verse: "I know that there is nothing better for men than to be happy and do good while they live" (Ecclesiastes 3:12). The passage goes on to say that it is a gift from God. Nothing better.

## A Gift from God

I hope you noticed that I like to cite studies that prove generosity of the kind I'm describing has long-lasting benefits for the giver. In earlier chapters we saw that gratitude, sharing, and encouragement produce physical and psychological rewards for the giver. This chapter is no different. Allan Luks undertook an extensive study of altruism in his book *The Healing Power of Doing Good: The Health and Spiritual Benefits of Helping Others.* Luks is the former executive director of the Institute for the Advancement of Health and executive director of Big Brothers Big Sisters of New York City. At one time

I served as the national ambassador for Big Brothers Big Sisters, though I never had the opportunity to meet Allan Luks.

Here's what an article on the Random Acts of Kindness Web site said about the study:

*Luks' study involved more than 3,000 volunteers of all ages at more than 20 organizations throughout the country. He sent a 17-question survey to these volunteers, asking them how they felt when they did a kind act. A total of 3,296 surveys were returned to Luks, and after a computerized analysis, he saw a clear cause-and-effect relationship between helping and good health. In a nutshell, Luks concluded, "Helping contributes to the maintenance of good health, and it can diminish the effect of diseases and disorders both serious and minor, psychological and physical."*

*The volunteers in Luks' study testified to feeling a rush of euphoria, followed by a longer period of calm, after performing a kind act. This feeling, which Luks calls "helper's high," involves physical sensations that strongly indicate a sharp reduction in stress and the release of the body's natural painkillers, the endorphins. This initial rush is then followed by a longer-lasting period of improved emotional well-being.*

I hope you got that.

Helping lessens the effects of both physical and mental disease, reduces stress, and gives you a rush of happiness. Sounds like the gift from God that the writer of Ecclesiastes was talking about.

## The Habit of Good Deeds

So how do we get in the habit of doing good deeds? Habits need to be cultivated. When I decided I wanted to do a daily good deed, I found myself looking for simple things that would brighten someone's day. The desire made me more intentional. I started looking for ways to show kindness.

I'm not saying it comes easily. We're all busy, distracted, and pulled in far too many directions. As with any habit, the more you practice, the more ingrained it will become. I second what John Wooden once said: "You can't live a perfect day without doing something for someone who will never be able to repay you."

And each time we perform some small act of kindness, we'll find ourselves rewarded by that rush of happiness and stress release. The very act offers its own reward and reinforces the behavior. That should be incentive enough.

## *Discovery*

*Cultivating the habit of good deeds will not only affect*
*those around us, it will improve our own emotional well-being.*

## Simple Good Deeds

So you've decided you want to join my good-deed-a-day club but you're stumped for ideas. Here's a list of kindness acts to get you started in brainstorming many more ideas of your own.

❖ *Do someone else's job.* It's as simple as that. If your husband does the dishes every night, surprise him by insisting he sit one night out while you clean up following dinner. Rake leaves for an elderly neighbor. Shovel the snow in front of your church, saving the janitor an added task. Or if you're the boss, you could offer to get coffee for someone who works for you.

❖*Be nice.* It's not complicated. If you're standing in a long line, replace impatience with a smile and a kind word or two. If you go to a restaurant, note the server's name and use it when addressing him or her. If travel plans get changed, smile and be kind to the agent having to rebook a whole planeload of people. Compliment a cute child to a proud parent or a well-behaved dog to an equally proud dog owner. Give up your seat to the elderly, hold doors for those coming behind you, stop for pedestrians, and wipe off the sink in a public restroom after you've used it. All these tiny acts add up.

❖ *Appreciate people.* Showing appreciation can take many forms. Drop notes to friends and acquaintances. Write a letter to a company to praise the service of one of their employees. Leave a generous tip to show appreciation.

❖ *Make a difference.* Some good deeds make a significant difference to those on the receiving end. If you live in farm country, you may be able to glean the fields and take the food to your soup kitchen or mission. Senior citizens can often use help with physical chores. Visit someone in jail. The key to doing good deeds that make a difference is keeping your eyes open for those in need.

❖ *Ask the Lord to nudge you.* Those "divine appointments" have often been the best way to see where I can help. If you are willing, God will lead you to those who need help.

*Bear with each other and forgive*

*whatever grievances you may have*

*against one another.*

*Forgive as the Lord forgave you.*

*Colossians 3:13*

# Five

# A Memory, a Guard, and an Outstretched Hand

## The Impact of Forgiveness

Okay, so there's nothing simple or easy about forgiveness—it may be one of the costliest gifts we're called upon to give. However, when we are committed to living in the spirit of generosity, forgiveness may very well be the gift that keeps on giving. If we are stingy with forgiveness, all our resources will begin to atrophy, shrivel, and eventually dry up.

We've talked about the physical benefits of gratitude, encouragement, and doing good deeds. Perhaps no gift we give will net as many benefits as offering the gift of forgiveness. Extensive research has been undertaken to study the effects of forgiveness and of unforgiveness as well.

In October 2003, more than forty top scientists from around the world who study forgiveness gathered in Atlanta to share their find-ings. The conference was hosted by A Campaign for Forgiveness Research, a nonprofit organization funded by grants from the John Templeton Foundation and the Fetzer Institute.

The presentations included the power of forgiving as it affects marriages, health, women, ethnic groups, religion, businesses, re-lationships, criminals and victims, substance abusers, and others. Some of the findings presented demonstrated that forgiveness was found to improve health. Those more forgiving of themselves and of others reported more life satisfaction. Forgiveness is a factor in low blood pressure. Forgiveness is linked to less depression. One of the studies demonstrated that among people who have chronic back pain, those who have forgiven others experience lower levels of pain and fewer associated psychological problems such as anger and depression than those who have not forgiven.

Evidence shows that a person who cannot or will not forgive will suffer long-term health problems. Forgiveness, on the other hand, lowers blood pressure, lowers the heart rate, lowers stress, reduces hostility, lessens the symptoms of depression, and lessens the symptoms of anxiety. It helps the person forgiving to manage anger, lowers the risk of alcohol and substance abuse, reduces chronic pain, improves psychological well-being, and leads to greater spiri-tual well-being.

I hope you're sitting up and taking notice because that's quite an impressive list. It doesn't end there, either. Those who forgive had more friends and healthier relationships. That's pretty amazing, isn't it? If forgiveness were a pill, it would be considered a miracle drug for all the beneficial effects it has on health and well-being.

When I think of forgiveness, my friend Jay immediately comes to mind. For as long as I've known Jay, he had worried over his younger sister, who has suffered from emotional and mental problems nearly her entire life. Let's call her Susie. More than once Susie has caused a major upheaval in the family.

Susie has disowned her family, including her own son and daughters, and sometimes cuts off communication for long periods of time. Yet she repeatedly returns, wanting to make amends. She's been in and out of the family more times than anyone can count. Each time she'd return sorry and apologetic, only the new attitude wouldn't last long. A few months or years later she'd have one of her episodes and make ugly, vicious claims against her siblings, then walk away disgusted with the lot of them.

Over the years she has written horrible letters and caused problems that cost untold amounts of emotional energy and sometimes thousands upon thousands of dollars. When last I heard of her, she lived in another town. No one knew exactly where she was or if she even had a home. Jay feared she was living on the streets.

But then out of the blue, yet predictably, Susie phoned. She said she'd been sitting in church and felt God was talking to her and saying, "You aren't the woman I thought you were. You need to reconcile with your family." And so she contacted her family.

Jay called to tell us. I could hear the excitement in his voice. After having watched Jay go through so many painful episodes with his sister, so many disappointments, I said, "Jay, don't you think you should be careful before you open yourself up to her? You know this has happened over and over again."

Jay was quiet for a time, and then he said the most beautiful thing: "I forgot to be mad at her."

His forgiveness was so complete that he forgot all about it. It was a wonderful lesson for me.

I don't think any story shows the power of forgiveness more than one told by Corrie ten Boom, the wonderful Christian woman I mentioned earlier. Corrie and her family secretly housed Jews in their home during World War II. When the Nazis discovered their activities, Corrie and her sister, Betsie, were sent to the German death camp Ravensbrück. There Corrie would watch many, including her sister, die. After the war she returned to Germany to declare the grace of Christ.

Here's the story of forgiveness in Corrie's own words from her book *Tramp for the Lord*:

*It was 1947, and I'd come from Holland to defeated Germany with the message that God forgives.*

*It was the truth that they needed most to hear in that bitter, bombed-out land, and I gave them my favorite mental picture. Maybe because the sea is never far from a Hollander's mind, I liked to think that that's where forgiven sins were thrown. "When we confess our sins," I said, "God casts them into the deepest ocean, gone forever. And even though I cannot find a Scripture for it, I believe God then places a sign out there that says, NO FISHING ALLOWED."*

*The solemn faces stared back at me, not quite daring to believe . . . And that's when I saw him, working his way forward against the others. One moment I saw the overcoat and the brown hat; the next, a blue uniform and a visored cap with skull and crossbones. It came back with a rush: the huge room with its harsh overhead lights, the pathetic pile of dresses and shoes in the center of the floor, the shame of walking naked past this man. I could see my sister's frail form ahead of me, ribs sharp beneath the parchment skin. Betsie, how thin you were!*

*That place was Ravensbrück, and the man who was making his way forward had been a guard—one of the most cruel guards.*

*Now he was in front of me, hand thrust out: "A fine message, Fräulein! How good it is to know that, as you say, all our sins are at the bottom of the sea!"*

And I, who had spoken so glibly of forgiveness, fumbled in my pocketbook rather than take that hand. He would not remember me, of course—how could he remember one prisoner among those thousands of women?

But I remembered him. I was face-to-face with one of my captors and my blood seemed to freeze.

"You mentioned Ravensbrück in your talk," he was saying. "I was a guard there." No, he did not remember me.

"But since that time," he went on, "I have become a Christian. I know that God has forgiven me for the cruel things I did there, but I would like to hear it from your lips as well. Fräulein"—again the hand came out—"will you forgive me?"

And I stood there—I whose sins had again and again to be forgiven—and could not forgive. Betsie had died in that place. Could he erase her slow terrible death simply for the asking?

It could have been many seconds that he stood there—hand held out—but to me it seemed hours as I wrestled with the most difficult thing I had ever had to do.

For I had to do it—I knew that. The message that God forgives has a prior condition: that we forgive those who have injured us. "If you do not forgive men their trespasses," Jesus says, "neither will your Father in heaven forgive your trespasses."

And still I stood there with the coldness clutching my heart.

But forgiveness is not an emotion—I knew that too. Forgiveness is an act of the will, and the will can function regardless of the temperature of the heart. "Jesus, help me!" I prayed silently. "I can lift my hand. I can do that much. You supply the feeling." And so woodenly, mechanically, I thrust out my hand into the one stretched out to me. And as I did, an incredible thing took place. The current started in my shoulder, raced down my arm, sprang into our joined hands. And then this healing warmth seemed to flood my whole being, bringing tears to my eyes.

*"I forgive you, brother!" I cried. "With all my heart!"*

*For a long moment we grasped each other's hands, the former guard and the former prisoner. I had never known God's love so intensely, as I did then. But even then, I realized it was not my love. I had tried, and did not have the power. It was the power of the Holy Spirit.*[1]

I've thought about that miracle of forgiveness many times since I first read Corrie's book. You can see that, once again, it's that miracle of multiplication. Corrie ten Boom says that forgiveness is not an emotion. It is an act of the will.

How wise. By lifting her hand in obedience, she was offering her own loaves and fishes, and a powerful miracle followed.

## Forgiveness as a Discipline

Martin Luther King, Jr., also recognized that forgiving is more than an emotional response. He said, "We must develop and maintain the capacity to forgive. He who is devoid of the power to forgive is devoid of the power to love. There is some good in the worst of us and some evil in the best of us. When we discover this, we are less prone to hate our enemies."[2]

I hope you caught these words: "develop and maintain the capacity." It sounds as if, according to Dr. King, forgiveness is a discipline that requires practice.

## The Reciprocity of Forgiveness

I love Søren Kierkegaard's prayer: "Father in Heaven! Hold not our sins up against us but hold us up against our sins so that the thought of You when it wakens in our soul, and each time it wakens, should not remind us of what we have committed but of what You did forgive, not of how we went astray but of how You did save us! Amen."[3]

In Matthew 6:14–15, Jesus says, "For if you forgive men when they sin against you, your heavenly Father will also forgive you. But if you do not forgive men their sins, your Father will not forgive your sins." Those are some chilling words, since we need the Lord's forgiveness to live.

One of my friends came to realize this with her sister. This sister had been unable to work because of health and emotional reasons for much of her life. She flirted with homelessness many times. This friend had helped her sister often through the years.

One time my friend actually bought her sister a new car and had made it possible for her sister to get a driver's license in the hope that it would give her a fresh start. Only later she found out that her sister had taken a loan using the car as collateral. The loan company repossessed the almost-new car for nonpayment of a small loan. Needless to say, my friend harbored resentment against her sister.

It was Christmas and my friend got a call from her mother. Apparently the sister was behind $800 on the rent. If she didn't have the money by the thirty-first of the month, she'd be evicted. My friend's mother had been widowed for thirty years and had all she could do to get by on her limited pension. It was up to my friend.

She fretted much of the night, alternating between praying and ranting. She and her husband always had enough to pay the bills, but there wasn't much left over. With a daughter in college, she knew she would have to blow the budget in order to help her sister. She could see no end. Her sister never paid back a single cent of the money she borrowed. My friend struggled with resentment.

The next morning she opened her Bible and her journal for her morning quiet time. She always planned her Bible readings in advance and jotted prayer requests in the left margin of her journal. On that morning's page she had written "Psalm 18" and, in the margin, a note to pray for her sister.

She read about the Lord as the Rock and the Deliverer. Next came a recounting of mighty things and how God delivered David from his enemies. Then she got to verse 20. "The Lord has dealt with me according to my righteousness; according to the cleanness of my hands he has rewarded me" (Psalm 18:20).

She took notes. "The Lord has dealt with me according to my righteousness. How righteous am I? I know the answer to that one—I'm not righteous at all. I am in need of a savior every single day. And how clean are my hands? They are only clean because His sacrifice—when He died in my place—cleansed them."

She prayed, especially praying for her sister, but couldn't stop worrying over the situation. She finally came to the conclusion that they'd give her sister the money but she'd have to admit to her chronic mismanagement. She remembers angrily thinking, *She's such a deadbeat; she doesn't deserve to be bailed out again.*

As she recounted, the voice in her head at that moment wasn't audible, but it was the nearest thing; *And do you think you deserve all that I've given you?*

My friend sat stunned. She realized this was not about her sister, it was about her.

Here's what she wrote in her journal: "The Lord had given us so much, yet when He offered the opportunity to give it back, I responded with the heart of a deadbeat. Sure I might have resentfully given her the money, but I withheld love, forgiveness, and acceptance—the most important gifts the Lord gave me. He gave me the very best, but when it was time to reciprocate, I squeaked out a miserly substitute."

After the Lord got my friend's attention, it didn't take her long to see this from His perspective. As she wrote in her journal, "This year, we will be giving a gift of $800 to Jesus on his birthday. He even told me where to send it. I pray the Lord will use this gift to speak to my sister."

## Final Form of Love

This poem written by Reinhold Niebuhr talks about how we were saved, tracing it to the final form of love, forgiveness:

Nothing worth doing is completed in our lifetime,
Therefore, we are saved by hope.
Nothing true or beautiful or good makes complete sense in any
immediate context of history;
Therefore, we are saved by faith.
Nothing we do, however virtuous, can be accomplished alone.
Therefore, we are saved by love.
No virtuous act is quite as virtuous from the standpoint of our
friend or foe as from our own;
Therefore, we are saved by the final form of love, which is
forgiveness.

### Discovery

*While it may not be a simple act, offering forgiveness not only has the power to heal relationships, it strengthens the well-being of those who give this life-changing gift.*

# A Not-So-Simple Act of Forgiveness

Today I drove behind a car bearing the license plate: 4GV 4GT. I'm guessing the plate meant "forgive and forget." Easy to put on a license plate, but forgiving is often one of the hardest things we are called to do. But the Lord doesn't ask us to do something he's not already done. And what's more, he promises to forgive us the very sins that caused him to be nailed to the cross. Read the promises that follow. If he can forgive us, can we do any less for others?

✦ The Lord is compassionate and gracious, slow to anger, abounding in love. He will not always accuse, nor will he harbor his anger forever; he does not treat us as our sins deserve or repay us according to our iniquities. For as high as the heavens are above the earth, so great is his love for those who fear him; as far as the east is from the west, so far has he removed our transgressions from us. As a father has compassion on his children, so the LORD has compassion on those who fear him. (Psalm 103:8–13)

✦ If we confess our sins, he is faithful and just and will forgive us our sins and purify us from all unrighteousness. (1 John 1:9)

✦ For he has rescued us from the dominion of darkness and brought us into the kingdom of the Son he loves, in whom we have redemption, the forgiveness of sins. Colossians (1:13–14)

❖ I write to you, dear children, because your sins have been forgiven on account of his name. (1 John 2:12)

❖ "Come now, let us reason together," says the LORD. "Though your sins are like scarlet, they shall be as white as snow; though they are red as crimson, they shall be like wool." (Isaiah 1:18)

❖Therefore, there is now no condemnation for those who are in Christ Jesus, because through Christ Jesus the law of the Spirit of life set me free from the law of sin and death (Romans 8:1–2)

*Whatever is true, whatever is noble,*

*whatever is right,*

*whatever is pure, whatever is lovely,*

*whatever is admirable*

*—if anything is excellent or praiseworthy—*

*think about such things.*

Philippians 4:8

# Six

# A Coach, a Cough Drop, and a Light Bulb

## The Power of Believing the Best

My friend's mother, Ruth, always believed the best about a person. The family teased her about it to no end. No matter who was mentioned, Ruth's face would soften and she'd say, "I think he must be a really nice person." The family would laugh, but there was something special inside her that assumed the best in everyone.

As far as the family was concerned, the real kicker came when Ruth sat quietly watching the news. A full-screen shot appeared of Osama bin Laden, the most notorious of all terrorists. Ruth spoke, almost to herself, "I just don't understand. He looks like such a nice person."

We all strive for discernment, but there's something about Ruth's brand of empathy and optimism that marks a person living in a spirit of generosity. In a world where criticism and cynicism have become national pastimes, there is nothing so generous as the person who sees you as God does.

The task is spelled out for us in 1 Peter 3:8–9. "Summing up: Be agreeable, be sympathetic, be loving, be compassionate, be humble. That goes for all of you, no exceptions. No retaliation. No sharp-tongued sarcasm. Instead, bless—that's your job, to bless. You'll be a blessing and also get a blessing" (*The Message*).

Wow, what a calling! And do you see how that verse ends with a double benefit—we will be a blessing and get a blessing. So again we come to the question: what's a chapter about empathy and believing the best about others doing in a book on generosity? Are you seeing the pattern yet, my friends? If we want to discover the power of generosity in our own lives, one of the most valuable gifts we can offer is seeing people in the best possible light. And here's where that multiplication comes in—when you believe the best about someone, they usually try hard to make your belief reality. Believe the best, be a blessing, receive a blessing.

## The Gift of Believing the Best

It's funny what will happen when you believe in the goodness of others. I've discovered that when you expect the best that's exactly what you get. People want to live up to what you think of them. When my son Ted was in high school, a gang of troublesome, threatening boys chose him as their victim. Ted had crossed them in some way. Once the principal actually sent Ted home for three days because he said he could not guarantee his safety at school. It was a scary time for Ted and our family. But there was this one classmate who befriended him who, oddly enough, was considered a troublemaker himself.

For some reason he connected with Ted. He'd reassure him, telling him not to worry about the bullies. "I've got your back, Ted," he'd say. His loyal friendship actually shielded Ted from much of the trouble.

Once when he came to our house I said, "Hey, buddy, I'm just grateful that you're there for Ted. You are a true friend." That one brief comment seemed to cement their friendship. The whole time they were friends the boy never let Ted down or gave us any reason to worry—he was a good friend. And he told my son, "You got a great mom, Ted. You got a great mom." I'm guessing this young man didn't get a lot of praise. When I recognized the best in him, that's exactly what he offered us—his very best.

Haddon W. Robinson told the following story in the *Christian Medical Society Journal*. On New Year's Day 1929, Georgia Tech played the University of California in the Rose Bowl. In that game a man named Roy Riegels recovered a fumble for California. Somehow, he became confused and started running. He ran sixty-five yards in the *wrong direction*. One of his teammates, Benny Lom, outdistanced him and downed him just before he scored for the opposing team. When California attempted to punt, Tech blocked the kick and scored a safety, which was the ultimate margin of victory.

That strange play came in the first half, and everyone who watched the game was asking the same question: "What will Coach Nibs Price do with Roy Riegels in the second half?" The men filed off the field and went into the dressing room. They sat down on the benches and on the floor, all but Riegels. He put his blanket around his shoulders, sat down in a corner, put his face in his hands, and cried like a baby.

If you have played football, you know that a coach usually has a great deal to say to his team during halftime. That day Coach Price was quiet. No doubt he was trying to decide what to do with Riegels. The timekeeper came in and announced that there were three minutes before playing time.

Coach Price looked at the team and said simply, "Men, the same team that played the first half will start the second." The players got up and started out, all but Riegels. He did not budge. The coach looked back and called to him again; still he didn't move. Coach Price went over to where Riegels sat and said, "Roy, didn't you hear me? The same team that played the first half will start the second."

Then Roy Riegels looked up and his cheeks were wet with a strong man's tears. "Coach," he said, "I can't do it to save my life. I've ruined you, I've ruined the University of California, I've ruined myself. I couldn't face that crowd in the stadium to save my life."

Coach Price reached out and put his hand on Riegel's shoulder and said to him: "Roy, get up and go on back; the game is only half over." And Roy Riegels went back, and those Tech men will tell you that they have never seen a man play football as Roy Riegels played that second half.[1]

I love that story. The coach may not have known 1 Peter 3:8–9, but he lived out those verses in the treatment of this young man. In Dr. Piero Ferrucci's book *The Power of Kindness*, Dr. Ferrucci quotes Aldous Huxley from a lecture he gave toward the end of his life. Huxley said, "People often ask me, what is the most effective technique for transforming their life. It is a little embarrassing that after years and years of research and experimentation, I have to say the best answer is—just be a little kinder."[2]

*Just be a little kinder.*

It sounds simple, but it may be one of the most difficult tasks. What is it that gives us the ability to see the best in people? Is it some form of saintly spirit? A natural altruism?

No. The trait is empathy—the ability to put one's self into someone else's shoes.

## *Discovery*

*Believing the best of others strengthens them
to live up to their best.*

## Empathy

Ruth, my friend's mother, was the champion of putting herself into other people's skins. Her stories were always peppered with, "Think of how he must've felt . . ." My friend remembers her mother telling the story of the first black girl who came to her small town. So vividly did her mother tell it, my friend says she has to remind herself that she never actually saw the small girl sitting alone on a far bench in the schoolyard. But day after day, according to Ruth, the girl would eat her Depression lunch fare—dry hush puppies out of a lard pail—while tears silently streaked her cheeks. No one spoke to her. Painfully shy herself, Ruth never approached the girl, who moved away after a time. Ruth never forgot the raw pain, nor did she ever stop regretting her own omission. That incident happened more than eighty years ago, yet every time Ruth told the story, you could feel that she still ached for that lonely young girl. That's empathy.

An interesting thing about empathy is that it often benefits the empathetic person as much as or more than those around him. *Giving aligns us to the heart of God.*

Studies have shown that empathetic people are more creative, more grateful, more satisfied, and less dogmatic. Interesting isn't it? Empathy—the abilities to understand, detect, and appropriately respond to the perspective and feelings of others—is the trait most closely linked to acts of heroism. Ervin Staub, himself a Holocaust survivor from Hungary, undertook extensive studies to find out what makes a hero—the person who will ignore personal peril to help someone else. He expected to find that the trait most evident in heroes was courage, but he was surprised to discover it was empathy.

Empathy may be the trait, but the outward expression of that trait is compassion.

## Compassion

Sitting in computer lab a few years ago, third-grader Austin Rosedale made a split-second decision that saved his teacher's life. Charisse Precht popped a cough drop into her mouth that somehow lodged in her throat, cutting off her air supply. According to an article by reporter David Hayes in the *Issaquah Press*, Ms. Precht dropped to her knees. As she felt herself fainting, she pointed to her throat and mouthed the word "Help."

Austin immediately came up behind his teacher, reached around her middle, and performed a perfect Heimlich maneuver, dislodging the cough drop and sending it flying across the room. When asked how the eight-year-old knew the Heimlich maneuver, Austin explained that he learned about it from his day planner, the last two pages of which included illustrations and descriptions of the technique. "I just visualized the pictures and remembered what I'd read," Austin said.

Austin's mother, Krissy Rosedale, says she isn't surprised at Austin's actions because caring is a part of her son's personality. She tells of the citizenship award he received last fall for befriending a new boy in town. "He's got compassion in him," she says. "He doesn't think anything of it, he just does it."

## Cultivating Optimism, Empathy, and Compassion

Before we can offer the gifts of compassion and empathy we need to figure out how to cultivate these traits. Think about it. If seeing the best in people is not something we're born with, then what are the techniques and practices that help us develop this perspective?

In 1913, the children's classic *Pollyanna*, by Eleanor Porter, was published. The book influenced generations of girls. It tells the story of a young orphan, Pollyanna, who moves to Vermont to live with her overcritical Aunt Polly. Pollyanna learned what she called the Glad Game from her missionary father, and it colored the way she viewed the world. The game consisted of trying to find something to be glad about in every situation. Throughout the story, Pollyanna's attitude becomes infectious and changes the lives of many of the town's inhabitants and eventually takes hold of the lone holdout, Aunt Polly.

In the Disney movie version of the story, Pollyanna wears a locket with a quote attributed to Abraham Lincoln: "When you look for the bad in mankind expecting to find it, you surely will." It's a great philosophy, though the writer of the film, not the president, created it.

But in this philosophy we uncover our technique. If you look for the bad in people, you'll find it. It's a simple matter of expectations. The Bible warns us to avoid this trap. In Philippians 4:8 it says, "Finally, brothers, whatever is true, whatever is noble, whatever is right, whatever is pure, whatever is lovely, whatever is admirable— if anything is excellent or praiseworthy—think about such things."

Consider it this way: we must control our thinking. Instead of being critical or snarky, which is the "in" thing to be, we can choose to adopt a Pollyanna attitude. We can practice the habit of finding the good in each person, in each situation. The verse above makes it clear that we need to direct our focus.

The list is a good one—whatever is true, noble, right, pure, lovely, admirable, excellent, and praiseworthy. It doesn't leave a lot of room for finding fault, criticizing, or questioning motives.

James Newton, in his book *Uncommon Friends,* tells a story about the famous inventor Thomas Edison: "Mr. Edison was working on a crazy contraption called a 'light bulb' and it took a whole team of men twenty-four straight hours to put just one together. The story goes that when Edison was finished with one light bulb, he gave it to a young boy helper, who nervously carried it up the stairs. Step by step he cautiously watched his hands, obviously frightened of dropping such a priceless piece of work. You've probably guessed what happened: the poor young fellow dropped the bulb at the top of the stairs. It took the entire team of men twenty-four more hours to make another bulb. Finally, tired and ready for a break, Edison was ready to have his bulb carried up the stairs. He gave it to the same young boy who dropped the first one."[4]

It doesn't take the light from one of Thomas Edison's bulbs to realize that he saw and expected the best in people.

It's the Whatever Principle at work, and it bears repeating—

whatever is true, noble, right, pure, lovely, admirable, excellent, and praiseworthy is what we need to focus our thoughts on.

As St. Vincent de Paul said, "Make it a practice to judge persons and things in the most favorable light at all times and under all circumstances."

That's a practice I want to cultivate in my life. Let's become abundantly generous in seeing people in the very best light. The light we offer may very well illuminate their pathway to take the very best next step. Now *that* is a gift worth giving.

## Discovery

*When we offer people the gift of believing the best of them, we light the pathway to their becoming the very best of who they are.*

## SIMPLE ACTS OF BELIEVING THE BEST

I f you want to be positive—to see the best in people— it will take practice. Habits can be difficult to break, especially the habit of seeing people in a critical light. Studies show that it takes about a month of constant vigilance to change a habit. Following are some tips to help you cultivate a generous outlook toward people.

◈ *Keep a journal.* I'm guessing that this suggestion comes as no surprise. You're probably ticking off the number of times

*(Continued)*

I've mentioned keeping a log of some kind. Let's see, a gratitude journal, a prayer journal, and now a journal to help you focus on seeing the positive in people. You can, of course, figure out a way to combine these into one life journal, but the act of writing things down, however you do it, helps greatly. By writing our intention to see the best in people, we're committing to a new quest. There's something powerful about writing our intentions. As you begin to find the good in people, write it down. Reinforce your victories.

❖ *Play Pollyanna's Glad Game.* Yes it seems simplistic, but there's real wisdom in looking for the good in every situation. Remember the benefits. We will be more creative, more grateful, more satisfied, and less critical.

❖ *Cover your intention with prayer.* When we ask God to help us live as He's asked us to live, we can expect an answer to that prayer.

❖ *Collect Bible verses.* The Bible is filled with verses encouraging us to see people as God sees them. Use your concordance and start collecting those verses. For starters, you might take a look at the book of Colossians, chapter 3. Write your favorite verses out in your journal. The very act of writing them helps us see them in a new light. Memorize them by repeating them often.

❖ *Be accountable.* Find someone you trust. Tell your friend that you're trying to see people in a more positive light. Ask her to nudge you every time she catches you falling back into old habits. Or better yet, enlist your friend to join you in your quest. You can hold each other accountable.

✤ *Commit for a month*. It takes a month or so to break a habit and develop a new one. Make a commitment for one month at a time. In your journal, you'll be tracking your progress. Keep track until you sense that you are ready to remove your training wheels.

✤ *Each time you fail, start over.* The Bible tells us we will fall short. Expect it. Confess it. Pick yourself up and start over again. As Ralph Waldo Emerson said, "Our greatest glory is not in never failing, but in rising up every time we fail."

Each man should give what he has

decided in his heart to give,

not reluctantly or under compulsion,

for God loves a cheerful giver.

2 Corinthians 9:7

## Seven

# Point Hope, a Piano Recital, and a House Yet to Come

### The Bounty of Open-Handed Giving

Elizabeth Peale Allen, in a letter to the Positive Thinkers Club, says, "A prerequisite to living abundantly is giving abundantly. These are two concepts that are woven tightly together. If you don't know how to give, you don't know how to live."

Go back and read that over again. We long to live abundantly—richly—but in order for that to happen, we first need to learn to give abundantly. It doesn't seem to make fiscal sense, but the Bible stresses this over and over. It's that ripple effect we've talked about. The power of multiplication.

I promised this book would be about more than opening our purses and wallets. Giving money is just one part of discovering the power of generosity. But being generous with our wealth is definitely an important part of what we are called to do.

## You Can Take It with You

You've heard the old saying that you can't take it with you. Well I disagree. We *can!* Listen to what the Bible says: "Tell those rich in this world's wealth to quit being so full of themselves and so obsessed with money, which is here today and gone tomorrow. Tell them to go after God, who piles on all the riches we could ever manage—to do good, to be rich in helping others, to be extravagantly generous. If they do that, they'll build a treasury that will last, gaining life that is truly life" (1 Timothy 6:18–19; *The Message*).

Look at that Bible verse again. God says we are to be extravagantly generous. Don't you love that term? In a world of stingy self-centeredness, we are called to be extravagantly generous. The verse says we will be building up a treasury that lasts. We are told to:

~ Go after God.

~ Do good.

~ Help others.

~ Be extravagantly generous.

Four little rules that will allow us to pile up real wealth and gain a life that is filled with riches. So how do we take it with us? Think of it this way. We are only in the world for a short time. We are an eternal people given a limited assignment on earth. If we don't want to blow this mission we will invest our money in people.

Those are the investments that will reap dividends when we get to heaven. And that's far better than a 401(k).

At the end of time, we will all stand before God. We are not going to be able to offer Him the luxury car or the vacation home. Those are nothing but dust in the eternal economy. Jesus will want to talk about the times we cared for widows and orphans, visited those in jail, or used our resources to reach the lost. Now I'm not saying the Lord doesn't shower us with gifts like cars and beautiful homes—sometimes He does. But He is far more interested in seeing what we do with the riches He piles on us. I remember the verse, "From everyone who has been given much, much will be demanded; and from the one who has been entrusted with much, much more will be asked" (Luke 12:48).

In the devotional book *New Every Morning,* authors D. James Kennedy and Jerry Newcombe said, "Money is nothing to God except an index to our souls."[1]

## *Use Money, Love People*

Pastor Rick Warren, in a sermon he preached at the annual Generous Giving Conference in Colorado Springs in 2005, said, "Money is to be used and not loved. You are to use money and you are to love people. If you get that reversed you are in trouble because if you start loving money, you will start using people to get more money."

I want to tell you about my friend Delilah, who is a radio personality. One of the reasons I'm drawn to her is that she gives with an open hand. But before I tell the story about how she lives in a spirit of generosity, I need to sidetrack a bit and tell you how we met. There's something of the miraculous in that.

I am a member of the Guideposts National Advisory Cabinet. They scheduled their annual meeting in the Seattle area in September 2008. Ted Nace, who was then the vice president of the board, asked if I could find a way to contact Delilah. He'd learned she lived in the Seattle area and felt I had better contacts than he did.

I laughed and said, "Ted, how am I supposed to meet Delilah? I have as much chance as you do. I don't know her. I listen to her on the radio, but I don't know her." He explained that he had written three letters, none of which she'd responded to. The cabinet wanted her to speak at the council meeting. He thought that if I, as a local person, contacted her on behalf of the board, I might have a better chance.

I felt bad about it because I would have loved to help, but I didn't have any way of getting in touch with her. I just whispered a little arrow prayer, "God, if you want me to meet Delilah, bring her into my life." So that was it.

I went off on a business trip. Whenever I come back from a trip, a mountain of mail and messages is piled on my desk. As I worked my way down to the bottom, I found a sticky note that said, "Somebody named Delilah came by your office to meet you."

I about fell over.

Heidi, who works in my office, had written the note. I went over to her, waving the note. "Delilah, the radio personality?"

Heidi, who was not familiar with Delilah said, "Well, I don't know, but my daughter seems to think so."

I e-mailed Delilah and she responded right away. When we met she said that her staff had been reading my books and really enjoyed them. She had just bought property in town and had moved to Port Orchard. When she found out I lived in the same town, she wanted to make the effort to meet me. She said she was confident we could be friends. She was right, and I treasure my association with her.

## *Point Hope*

One of the many things I admire about Delilah is her heart. She does her radio show from her home, where she has a houseful of adopted children. One night, she was talking on the air, taking requests, and reading e-mail. She clicked on an e-mail that looked like one of the scams we receive all too often. The sender said she was a woman in a refugee camp in Ghana who desperately needed money to feed her three siblings and her son. Delilah was poised to delete it when she saw the line that said someone had mentioned that Delilah adopted African-American children and might be willing to help an African family. Delilah stopped. How could a spammer know that?

She quickly wrote back to ask for details. As it turned out, the woman was real. Her name was Winifred and she lived at the Buduburam refugee camp. She didn't have access to a computer and couldn't write in English and had asked her cousin to contact Delilah on her behalf.

Delilah didn't know how it was possible to help or how to go about getting money to Africa. Another question was how to tell if the need was real. The solution came in her association with World Vision. She knew the organization would be able to supply the answer. With the simple stroke of a few computer keys, she forwarded her e-mails to them with the request to investigate and report back if the request was authentic.

Not only was World Vision able to find Winifred, the organization learned that her siblings had indeed escaped the civil war in Liberia, were packed into a refugee camp in Ghana, and were starving. World Vision had a staffer familiar with that very camp. They asked Delilah to come to the World Vision offices for a meeting.

Delilah sat down with a group from the charitable organization and said, "I'd like to sponsor this family. I want them to have food and a place to live." They worked out the details and she got up to leave.

One of the men quietly spoke up. "You've just helped five people. What about the other forty-two thousand?"

Delilah laughed, shrugged her shoulders, and as she walked out of the conference room she said, "That's not my problem. They didn't write to me."

Delilah still tears up when she recalls that moment. She says that as soon as she left the room, God stopped her in her tracks. She couldn't believe she'd replied in such a flippant manner. She turned on her heel and returned to the room. "Forgive me for saying that. What can I do?"

That one question started an avalanche in Delilah's life and in the lives of 42,000 war refugees in Ghana. The first thing she did was travel to Africa to see conditions for herself. Then she rolled up her sleeves and got to work.

Realizing that water meant life in Ghana and there was no freshwater source in the camp, she started a ministry called Point Hope. Since Delilah's initial visit in 2004, Buduburam has twelve new pumping stations for clean water. With the water they are now able to produce food. They have tilapia fishponds and vegetable gardens. There's even a clinic complete with medical staff. Winifred, the woman who first contacted Delilah, started her own successful hair-braiding business. Delilah visits Buduburam regularly. She is blessed with riches that have nothing to do with money. All it took was a willing heart and an open hand.

## *Gifts Multiplied and Returned*

Delilah's gift has multiplied by thousands. When we give, it often comes back to us multiplied—like the little boy's loaves and fishes.

I am encouraged by the story of two young men working their way through Stanford University in 1892. Their funds got desperately low, and the idea came to one of them to engage Ignacy Jan Paderewski for a piano recital and earmark the profits for their board and tuition. The great pianist's manager asked for a guarantee of two thousand dollars. The students, undaunted, proceeded to stage the concert. They worked hard, only to find that the concert had raised only sixteen hundred dollars. After the concert, the students sought the great artist and told him of their efforts and results. They gave him the entire sixteen hundred dollars and accompanied it with a promissory note for four hundred dollars, explaining that they would earn the amount at the earliest possible moment and send the money to him. "No," replied Paderewski, "that won't do." Tearing the note to shreds, he returned the money and said to them, "Now, take out of this sixteen hundred dollars all of your expenses, and keep for each of you ten percent of the balance for your work, and let me have the rest."

The years rolled by—Paderewski had become prime minister of Poland. The devastating war came, and Paderewski was striving to feed the starving in his beloved Poland. There was only one man in the world who could help Paderewski and his people. Thousands of tons of food began to come into Poland for distribution by the Polish prime minister.

After the starving people were fed, Paderewski journeyed to Paris to thank Herbert Hoover for the relief sent to him. "That's all right, Mr. Paderewski," was Mr. Hoover's reply. "Besides, you don't remember it, but you helped me once when I was a student at college and I was in a hole."[2]

## Discovery

*We never know how our acts of open-handed giving are going to be used and multiplied by God, but we can be certain that they will be.*

## Listening for Those God Nudges

I'm not saying it's easy to know where to put our financial resources. Of course the church comes first. We need to give back the tithe to the church—that doesn't belong to us in the first place. I'm talking about the giving over and above our tithe. Sometimes it's difficult to discern the real needs. Delilah solved this by going to World Vision, a trusted organization. We have to remember that very often the ones asking loudest are not the ones the Lord would have us support. Again, it's a matter of listening for that nudge from Him. And sometimes we just step out there.

When I'm on a book tour I am generally met at the airport by what is known as a media escort. This is someone the publisher hires to pick me up and take me where I'm supposed to go. I have always been met on time except for once. For the first time in my twenty-plus-year career as a writer, the media escort did not show up at the airport.

Okay, I'm a big girl, I knew the name of the hotel, I figured I could find a taxi and make my own way there. I lugged my suitcase outside and headed for the transportation line. As I joined the queue, a businessman cut in front of me just as I reached the front. However, his cell phone rang and he stopped briefly to answer it. Thinking he would take the first cab I automatically went to the second. The driver got out and hoisted my fifty-pound suitcase into his trunk. Just then the attendant came up and said, "No, no, no. He hasn't gotten into a car." He pointed at the businessman, who was still on his cell phone. "You need to go in the first car." So the poor driver had to lift my heavy suitcase out of the trunk and lug it over to the big SUV in the front of the line. And just as big was the woman who was driving it.

After I climbed into the car, recited my destination and the address, the driver pulled away from the curb. Trying to be friendly, I asked, "How are you today?"

She sighed long and said, "Oh, I'm just the devil's target." I could see that she had a Bible on her seat.

"What do you mean by that?"

"Well, the devil's just out to get me." And she went on to tell me this whole litany of things that were going wrong in her life. Her husband had died. Her son who had a drinking problem had disappeared. And she was losing her house. She had been doing everything she could to try to make up the house payments, but because of some questionable charges and some dubious financial side-stepping by the mortgage company, she just couldn't get on top of it. It was a long, complicated story.

About five minutes into the conversation it just hit me that God had put me in that cab for a reason. I said, "What you need is an attorney to help you settle this."

She gave a brief laugh. "Oh, yeah, like I can afford an attorney."

I said, "You may not be able to afford one, but I can."

She was going sixty-five miles an hour down the freeway, but she whipped her head around and stared at me. "Did God send me an angel?"

I got her information before she dropped me off at the hotel. After I checked in, I went down to the concierge. "I need an attorney."

He looked up. "What kind of attorney do you need?"

"A mean one. I want an O.J.-mean one."

He talked to a couple of people and he came back with a name. And as I sat in my hotel room I prayed and asked, "Lord, am I doing the right thing? Is this what you want me to do?" I needed a confirmation.

I phoned the attorney the concierge had suggested to me, but apparently he was out for lunch and the answering service picked up. I left a message and was assured someone would return my call. A half hour later, his legal assistant reached me. "Debbie Macomber? Is this the writer?"

That was my confirmation.

## Giving That Reflects the Giver

We're called to give our best. The story is told that one day a beggar by the roadside asked for alms from Alexander the Great as he passed by. The man was poor and wretched and had no claim upon the ruler, no right even to lift a hopeful hand. Yet the king threw him several gold coins. A courtier was astonished at his generosity and commented, "Sir, copper coins would adequately meet a beggar's need. Why give him gold?" Alexander lifted his head and responded, "Copper coins would suit the beggar's need, but gold coins suit Alexander's giving."

I keep thinking about how my giving can suit my work. When the publisher Leisure Arts came to me, asking if they could do a pattern book based on my first book, *The Shop on Blossom Street,* it seemed like a perfect opportunity to give. I'm not a designer, so the only thing that I was contributing to this project was my name and my passion for knitting. I wouldn't have to do anything to earn this money; it would just be gravy. What better way to use that money than to give it back. I made arrangements for my royalties to go to charitable knitting organizations. Later, when the knitting notions line was launched, Wayne and I decided that all my portion of the royalties would go to World Vision. I worked out projections and figured the amount that I could expect to net. God surprised me again. He multiplied that projected number more than tenfold.

## What Can I Do?

I also receive money from my merchandising efforts. This too is separate from my income from books. I earmark this for children.

I've become friends with Damian, the young man who owns the car service in our town. He's a social worker by day and runs his car service in the off-hours. He picked me up at the airport a few months ago, and I noticed how discouraged he was. It's not like him to be discouraged.

"I don't think I can do this anymore," he said about his job as a social worker. "I think I'm going to have to quit my job." He told me what had led to his feeling of hopelessness. He had had to remove two preschool children from a home. The mother had chosen to live with a man who was a convicted sex abuser and child abuser. The state had decreed that if she chose to live with this man, it would have no option but to take the children away. She moved in with the abuser anyway. And so Damien had to take these two children, three and four years old, out of the home. They were traumatized, and worse, there was no place for them to go. They spent the entire day in the hallway outside of Social Services. Not only did he have to take these precious children away from their mother, but eventually he had to separate the children. It just broke his heart.

Earlier, I had come across the story of Richard Paul Evans. He wrote a book called *The Christmas Box*. I am inspired by how this book came about. It was Christmas, and Richard, who was unemployed at the time, didn't have a lot of money for gifts. Instead, he wrote a Christmas story to give to his family. He printed it out, stapled it together, and gave it as his gift to his brothers and sisters. They loved it and started sharing it with other people. Rick began getting phone calls from people who had read the story. They were sobbing, telling him how much they loved it. So he printed more. He sold 2,600 copies of this first edition—self-published, copied, and stapled together. He made several thousand dollars on it. Simon & Schuster heard about it and offered to publish the book. His first royalty check was $4 million. It's hard to imagine how many copies sold to earn that large a royalty check. Rick stared at that check and was afraid the money would ruin him. Being a godly man, he prayed and asked God, "What can I do?"

God always seems to have an answer when we ask that question. Richard Paul Evans built a facility for at-risk children called the Christmas Box House. I toured it. It has a medical facility, a dentist, classrooms, and private rooms for the children. It has an area for supervised visitation. The whole community got behind the Christmas Box House.

Ironically, when Damien picked me up that day, I had been to a fundraiser for the Christmas Box House in Salt Lake City. And then I came home to find out how desperately we needed one in my area. Damien was discouraged, but his experience birthed a dream. I'm hoping somehow, someway, to get a home here in Kitsap County for these kids—a warm, welcoming clearinghouse for children in crisis.

Damien and I are working on it.

I'm not saying you need to take on a family in Africa or build a home for children—those assignments are taken. All you have to do is open your hands and ask God, "What can I do?"

If you want to take it with you when you die, it's a surefire recipe for success.

## *Discovery*

*Forget what the world says; you **can** take it with you.*

---

### SIMPLE ACTS OF OPEN-HANDED GIVING

❖ Give to your local church first before expanding your universe of giving.

❖ I shared some stories with you about sensing God nudging me to help an individual. Those are wonderful opportunities, but this is the exception for me rather than the rule. Giving can usually be optimized best when done through a well-respected charity.

❖ Don't be afraid to check out organizations you want to help to ensure ethical fund-raising and administration practices.

❖ Sometimes needs can be overwhelming. The need is often far greater than our resources. Don't be afraid to be strategic. Normally you'll want time to think about opportunities. Don't be afraid to push the pause button while you do some research and look into the organization or individual. We are called to be wise as well as generous.

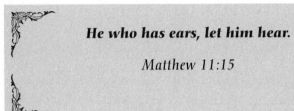

He who has ears, let him hear.

*Matthew 11:15*

# Eight

# *Static, Stories, and Chow-Chow*

## *The Art of Listening*

A storyteller needs to be a careful listener.

When people speak, I listen, because little pieces of their conversations may give me a story idea or even become part of a book. I learned a valuable lesson about listening from my mother. For many years my mother and I talked every day on the phone. We'd talk about this person or that event, about my kids and grandkids. Sometimes we'd just reminisce together. But one day she surprised me. Out of the blue she asked, "So, Debbie, how are your bowels?" The question was so unexpected; it just cracked me up.

"Mom, what do you mean?" I asked as I struggled to keep from laughing.

"Well, your bowels are important," she said without so much as a pause.

After I hung up the phone I wondered why in the world my mother would ask me such a question.

Then it hit me. Mom was worried about her own digestive system but didn't know how to put that concern into words. That's when I realized an important truth—*we ask people questions we long to have them ask us.* It gave me a whole new perspective on listening to others.

You might ask why we're discussing listening in a book about discovering the power of generosity. Can you think of a more important gift than the art of listening? The Greek philosopher Epictetus said, "Nature gave us one tongue and two ears so we could hear twice as much as we speak." That is still good advice.

## Be Quiet

Helen H. Cepero, former director of spiritual formation at North Park Theological Seminary, shared the following story in *The Covenant Companion:*

*During my morning lap swim, as I followed the rhythm of lift, breathe, and kick, the words came to me with utter clarity, "Be quiet, just shut up." A few more laps, and the words returned, "Be quiet."*

*I had begun my swim that day remembering that I had a morning appointment with a student who very likely did not want to meet with me at all. Samantha sat in the back corner of the classroom at North Park Theological Seminary where I taught spiritual direction. Often arriving late, she sat with her arms crossed, her manner radiating sincere hostility. Today she would meet with me for our first spiritual direction time together, not because she chose to, but because it was*

*required of her to pass the class. Recalling this meeting with some
dread I again heard the words, "Be quiet."*

*An hour later I was sitting across from Samantha and decided to
follow what seemed to be a clear instruction to say nothing. I simply
admitted, "I really know nothing about you, Samantha. What is your
story?"*

*That's almost all I said for the next hour. In the time that fol-
lowed my opening question Samantha told me about living in the
Bronzeville neighborhood on the South Side of Chicago. She talked
about the kids on the street corners and her efforts to befriend them.
She told me about raising her family in the neighborhood and some
of the pitfalls and threats that faced her own children. Then after
a moment of more silence she told me about her own growing-up
years and her abusive stepfather and her stormy relationship with a
mother who did not protect Samantha from her husband's sexual ad-
vances. At one point, I just sighed out the words, "Wow—that sounds
so hard." She simply nodded.*

*Then Samantha told me about her husband whom she loved deeply
and the marriage ministry they shared together with couples whose
marriages were struggling. I heard too about the gift of her faith and
how her relationship with Jesus sustained her through all that had
happened to her in the past and what she was experiencing right now
in her life. I smiled as this story of hope unfolded out of such difficult
circumstances.*

*When I told her our time together was nearly over, Samantha asked
if she could pray. After praying, she looked up at me and said, "Well,
that was not nearly as bad as I expected!" I asked if I could give her a
hug, knowing that a barrier had broken down between us. I wondered
how long it had been since she had told her story to someone else. I
knew that I felt honored and privileged to be her listener that morning.*[1]

## Statistically Speaking

Studies show that the lion's share of what we know we learned through listening. How sad that we are probably listening at only about a 25 percent comprehension rate. Think how much more we'd know if we could improve our listening.

According to HighGain, a company that specializes in training clients to listen, on average we listen at about 125 to 175 words per minute, but we listen at rates up to 450 words per minute.[2] This could be the reason we don't focus 100 percent on the person speaking. We're thinking circles around his or her words, causing us to retain precious little. When questioned, most people could only recall about 50 percent of what was said immediately after listening.

If all that is true, no wonder there is so much miscommunication. So the question becomes, how can I listen better? And maybe an even more important question—why is it important to listen?

## Why Is It So Difficult to Listen?

We need to work harder at listening than ever before. Why? Because we live in a static-filled world. The media blasts us with messages 24/7. Our televisions are turned on far more than we'd like to admit. All too frequently we listen to a child or a spouse with only half an ear so as not to miss what's being said on TV.

How often have you seen someone engaged in a lively conversation when her cell phone rings? Then she ignores the friend to carry on a conversation with an unseen third party while the friend twiddles his thumbs and waits. What does that do to the real-time conversation . . . or the friendship, for that matter?

Then there are computers. Too many of us are so engaged with e-mail or Web activities that we neglect interacting with those around us. Face it: we are a culture with earbuds crammed into our ear canals, dancing to a tune no one else hears.

If we are going to be committed to listening—really listening—we are going to have to turn off the media and tune out distractions.

And it's not just the commotion going on around us, either. Listening takes time and effort. If we want to listen, really listen, we can't be rushed. In our hurry-up, can't-we-cram-in-just-one-more-thing society, it's getting more and more difficult to find time to listen. An impatient, out-of-time listener often repeatedly interrupts the person speaking in an effort to speed up the process.

Good listening requires focusing on the other person rather than on ourselves and our own thoughts or reactions. Too many of us have a habit of spending much of our listening time composing what we're going to say next. That makes it nearly impossible to listen well.

## Why Do We Need to Listen?

The act of being generous with our listening is a gift that our world is longing to receive. Can you imagine the reasons this is true? For one thing, in our isolated world, people long to be heard. From the moment we enter school we are encouraged to participate—to talk, to share opinions, to give answers. But with everyone caught up in expressing his or her own thoughts and feelings, there are far too few listeners to hear. The bottom line is that when we take the time to really listen, others feel valued. What a wonderful gift to be able to give. And best of all, it's free!

According to behavioral studies, we benefit when we listen. Generous listening improves our own sense of well-being. It's one of those curious things. We can easily see how talking—self-expression—would improve our sense of satisfaction, but listening? Yet it is true. When we give this gift, we are giving ourselves a gift as well.

While we're talking about the benefits of listening, here's another one. Listening increases wisdom. We can learn about our surroundings and how we fit in with others. Listening helps us to define ourselves. We learn about who we are and how others perceive us by keeping our ears open and our mouths shut. All are vital lessons that we miss if we don't take time to listen. And, unfortunately, too often we don't.

My friend serves on the board of her church. They had been dealing with a number of tough issues when it came time for the annual board retreat. Few wanted to spend twenty-four hours looking at ministry models and talking about relevance and change. And to be honest, my friend confessed, very few—including her—wanted to spend any time with one another after so many contentious meetings. She figured it would be precious hours spent on nothing but blah, blah, blah.

Was she ever surprised!

Instead of planning work sessions, the only thing on the agenda was for each member to tell his or her story. The pastor went first and told how as a little boy growing up in Japan, the son of missionary parents, he had to go to boarding school when he was only six years old. He shared that he was so homesick, he cried every day for three years. Whenever his parents took him back to school, he'd hang on to the gate, crying as they left.

When he finished his story, not a person there could hide his or her tears. The vulnerability set the stage for story after story. Except for the brief time my friend told her story, she spent the entire retreat listening. She says it was the most powerful session they ever had. And that listening and understanding has spilled over into everything their board has done. They may still be wrestling with some perplexing issues, but because they listened to one another—really listened—there's a new unity, a deep respect and love. It's being multiplied throughout their church as well. It's that ripple effect.

## *Discovery*

*Becoming generous in listening can transform our relationships.*

## Listening by Asking Questions

The interchange with my mother taught me to listen to the questions people ask so I can understand what they are thinking about. Asking questions also helps me discover how to connect with people. I practice listening for the question they ask of me so I can turn it around and ask them back. It's the secret of knowing what people want to talk about.

Try it at a social event. When someone asks you, "So what do you do for a living?" or "How many grandchildren do you have?" or "Are you a football fan?" answer the question and then ask it right back. You'll probably find that your friend's face will light up and he'll happily launch into the subject. The plus of practicing this small experiment is that it's easier to get past the surface conversation. It helps reveal the other person's passions. What a genuine gift it is to put someone at ease.

The funny thing is that the more intentionally you listen, the more you will be considered a great conversationalist.

Of course, I'm not saying this is easy. You would think I'd have learned to listen to the questions my mother asked, but every once in a while I'd miss hearing what lurked behind her comments. One time during our daily phone visit she said, "Do you ever watch Jack LaLanne?"

"No, Mom," I said, "I'm writing during that time."

"Oh." She paused. "He's got a juicer he's selling."

"Well, Mom, do you want me to buy you that juicer?"

"No, Debbie," she said. "It's much too expensive. I don't think that's a wise way for you to spend your money."

Being wise with money was important to my mom and dad, so I dropped it. The next day we were talking again and she said, "I was watching Jack LaLanne again, and I was just thinking, that juicer just might help your father's bowels." Clearly bowels were of utmost importance to my mother.

"Mom, do you want me to buy you that juicer?"

"No, no, no, it's just way too expensive." My mother never forgot her Depression-era roots, so I knew she couldn't get past the price.

The next day during our call she brought it up again. "I was just thinking, if I had that juicer, I could make that chow-chow you like so well."

"What is chow-chow, Mom?"

"You like it!"

"You know, Mom," I said, "I just think I'd better get you that juicer."

And of course she said, "No, no, no, it's way too expensive."

This time I got the message. I ordered her the juicer. We need to listen past the protestations sometimes and recognize the desire.

It's not surprising that Jesus spent much of His time drawing people out with questions. "Who do you think I am?" or "Have you understood these things?" Did you know that in the Gospel of Matthew alone, Jesus asked close to a hundred questions?

## Listening to God

When we begin to listen to people, we also need to tune our ear to God on their behalf. In his book *Prayer: Finding the Heart's True Home*, Richard Foster says: "First we listen. This is the step of discernment. We listen to people and we listen to God. Sometimes people share their deepest needs in the most casual, offhand way. But if we are listening, really listening, there is often a rise within us, an inner 'yes,' which is a divine invitation to prayer."

Being a writer, I've always kept journals, written prayers, and de-voted much of my study time to the written word. Each morning I rise early. I enjoy being up long before anyone is stirring. The house is quiet and the world is dark. I read my Bible and I read from a series of much-loved and well-worn devotional books. My goal is to read the entire Bible from cover to cover each year. With so many wonderful translations available I read a new one each year.

When I'm finished with my Bible reading, I write out my prayers in longhand in a prayer journal. This helps keep me focused on my prayers and doesn't allow my mind to wander. During all that study and devotional writing, the hardest thing is to make time to be still and listen.

Sometimes I wonder what God thinks of our prayers. We praise Him, we confess our sins and shortcomings, we ask Him to step in and help us, we pray for others, we thank Him, and we just talk.

And talk.

And talk.

Unfortunately, we are not a listening people. The ability to listen comes hard for most of us, but we need to practice the same listen-ing skills in our relationship with God as we do with other people. Think about how difficult it is to keep from interrupting when we feel we have something important to say. It's important to maintain eye contact, to listen for the unspoken things, and ask questions.

God wants us to listen to Him. "If my people would but listen to me" (Psalm 81:13). And how many times do we hear Jesus saying, "He who has ears, let him hear" (Matthew 11:15).

Practice listening long enough to recognize the voice of God. When Elijah listened for God's voice, it didn't come in a dramatic way. "And he said, go forth, and stand upon the mount before the Lord. And, behold, the Lord passed by, and a great and strong wind rent the mountains, and brake in pieces the rocks before the Lord;

but the Lord was not in the wind: and after the wind an earthquake; but the Lord was not in the earthquake: and after the earthquake a fire; but the Lord was not in the fire: and after the fire a still small voice" (1 Kings 19:11–12; King James Version).

Yes, a still small voice.

It takes careful listening to hear that still small voice.

Thomas Merton said, "Silence is the first language of God; all else is a poor translation."

Remember when I said that giving aligns us to the heart of God? Listening is one of those gifts that puts us in sync with Him. Just as He listens, we need to listen to others. When I seek to discover the power of generosity, I want to be a generous listener.

An extravagantly generous listener.

## *Discovery*

*When we are generous listeners, we will gain far more than we give.*

## Simple Acts of Listening

✦ Are you an appreciative listener? Nodding occasionally and smiling demonstrates that you are connected with the speaker, appreciating what she has to say.

✦ Are you an engaged listener? If you practice active listening skills like leaning forward and making eye contact, the person speaking will feel as if he's been heard and you will grasp more of what's being said.

✦ Are you an intuitive listener? As much as 75 percent of all communication is nonverbal. Pay attention to all the signals.

Words are just part of the message; try to hear the ideas and feeling behind the words. Listen for the unspoken. You'll be amazed at what you discover.

✠ Are you an empathetic listener? When you strive for a respectful understanding of the person speaking you move away from a critical form of listening or a fix-it mentality. An empathetic listener uses his imagination to put himself in the speaker's shoes.

✠ Do you withhold the gift of listening? Many habits will render our best intentions worthless. Here are some habits to recognize and break in order to become a generous listener:

*Interrupting.* It takes real discipline to keep from interrupting, especially if the conversation is exciting or is dragging on. Work hard at listening to the entire thought.

*Story stealing.* That's when you try to top the speaker's story with one of your own: "If you think *that* is something . . ."

*Jumping ahead.* It can be a temptation to finish the speaker's sentence, but it's another way to pull back the gift of listening.

*Breaking eye contact.* Have you ever been talking to someone who seems to be looking around for someone more interesting? Nothing diminishes the speaker more that when he senses you are not connected.

*Getting off track.* Asking for details can sometimes be a form of active listening, but if you keep sidetracking the story, it does just the opposite.

*Be joyful in hope, patient in affliction,*

*faithful in prayer.*

*Share with God's people who are in need.*

*Practice hospitality.*

Romans 12:12–13

# Nine

# Jambalaya, Cupcakes, and the North Platte Canteen

## The Practice of Hospitality

The most generous people I know open their doors wide and work hard to make guests feel comfortable in their homes. When we are generous in hospitality, we open the door for so many simple acts of generosity. I like to think of hospitality as an invitation to God to use me in the lives of others.

Some of you may cringe at the mention of hospitality. If you are a perfectionist about your house and about meals, it may be hard to relax enough to enjoy the free and easy camaraderie that comes with having guests, both invited and impromptu. But offering hospitality is a matter of loaves and fishes—we simply offer what we have. Perhaps the ultimate act of hospitality in the Bible is the feeding of five thousand with nothing more than a child's lunch. It's the multiplication that makes it a miracle.

## Simple Hospitality

I was talking about hospitality with a much-traveled friend. She's been invited as a guest to some of the finest restaurants in our country and has been offered hospitality by friends whose home was featured in *Architectural Digest* and others who employ their own private chef. She's enjoyed unforgettable meals by some who are gourmet cooks themselves. She's dined at tables with hand-embroidered linens, crystal, and fine china, but when I asked her to describe the perfect kind of hospitality, she didn't hesitate. "It's my friends, Bob and Mary Martin."

Her face lit up as she spoke. "Their house is always open. If we are going to be in their vicinity around six o'clock, we know there'll be enough food and wonderful company." Bob Martin loves to cook and often makes up an oversized stockpot filled with chili or gumbo. The pot goes onto a trivet in the middle of the table and colorful bowls are set out. A big salad and pans of homemade cornbread may complete the fare. Guests often bring something to add to the meal. The first few who show up get the chairs around the table. If there's an overflow, other seating arrangements are made. The stragglers might find themselves perched on the kitchen stool with the breadboard pulled out as an impromptu table. Guests include Mary's aged parents, friends, grandchildren, choir members, and business associates—it's usually as eclectic a mix of people as it is of food. If it looks like the supply is running low, leftovers come out of the refrigerator and are heated up. "The best part," says my friend, "is the conversation and laughter around that table. I've met some of the most interesting people over Bob Martin's stroganoff or jambalaya."

It doesn't take fancy linens to offer hospitality. Bowls of popcorn and table games or a great movie can be just as much fun. Take inventory of your own loaves and fishes. We each have something to offer.

## Hospitality Family Style

Have you got a backyard? Can you grill hot dogs? Perfect! People rarely invite families over anymore. With our four rambunctious kids, people almost never invited us to dinner, but when they did, the kids would get so excited they could hardly contain themselves. Wayne had an aunt—actually his mother's cousin, but she was Aunt Margaret to us. She loved my kids. When she came to visit or asked us to her home it was like Christmas and birthday rolled into one. I remember one day, Ted was so excited that when Aunt Margaret walked inside the house he ran circles around her four times. She laughed and asked, "Is he always this happy?"

What joy it brings, especially to people with young children, just to invite them for a meal or dessert. It means the world to them, and it gives the parents a break, too. Look around your church or around your neighborhood. Is there a family who'd enjoy that back-yard wiener roast? My guess is yes.

One of my friends is an empty-nester but she loves to mix it up. When she entertains a young couple with children, she has the children go into the kitchen after dinner to prepare dessert. She prepares unfrosted cupcakes or plain cookies and has every kind of icing, confectioner's candy, and decoration a child could want.

The children are told to create masterpieces for each guest with prizes going to the winners in a number of categories. (Of course every child will be a winner in one category or another.) The adults are winners as well because they get to visit couple to couple while listening to the children laughing and creating happily in the next room.

## The North Platte Canteen

Because my father was a World War II veteran, I've always loved the story of the hospitality of North Platte, Nebraska. During World War II, 6 million American soldiers passed through North Platte on troop trains en route to their ultimate destinations in Europe and the Pacific. Can you imagine? The little town decided they wouldn't let the GIs come through without offering them hospitality. They transformed their modest railroad depot into the North Platte Canteen. Ask any serviceman who rolled through North Platte about the canteen and you'll find men who tear up as they describe the frightened boys of more than half a century ago who found warmth and comfort from the citizens there.

The volunteers kept the canteen open from early morning until the last train left the station after midnight. The project was staffed and funded entirely by the people of North Platte. The town barely tipped the scales at twelve thousand people, but they were able to offer snacks and treats, baskets of food and warm hugs and prayers to more than 6 million soldiers by the time the last troop train rolled through the town.

## The Hospitality Mandate

It's obvious that some people have the gift of hospitality, like the Martins. Not many of us could open our homes to friends with little notice. But all of us, gifted or not, are called to entertain. "Offer hospitality to one another without grumbling" (1 Peter 4:9). Throughout history, hospitality has been absolutely necessary. In most cultures, offering hospitality to strangers was expected. Once a traveler was sheltered under your roof, your responsibility was to care for his needs and offer protection. Those traveling had little option but to depend on the kindness of strangers for shelter, whether it was a home, a Bedouin tent, or even a stable.

*Philoxenia*, the Greek word for hospitality, literally means "loving strangers." Even today, offering hospitality is more than a nicety—it's a biblical mandate.

## Martha Stewart I Am Not

When Wayne and I were first married, we had four kids in a nine-hundred-square-foot house, but we made sure our home was as welcoming to our children's friends as we could make it. Now I'll admit—I'm not the best housekeeper in the world, and at times it kept me from being comfortable inviting people over. Looking back, I wish it hadn't.

Nobody is going to come into your home and start running a finger over surfaces to see how much dust you have on the coffee table. And if they're that judgmental, they need the gift of love and hospitality more than anyone else. Invite them over, hand them a dustcloth, and just surround them with acceptance and love.

I wonder if that discomfort comes from thinking we should be superwomen. My mother, who loved offering hospitality and entertained frequently, was a meticulous housekeeper. Meticulous, oh my goodness. I can remember one time when she came to visit. She walked straight to the microwave and looked inside and said, "Ah ha, I knew it! You're not cleaning your microwave."

I did the best I could to live up to my mother's example with four little ones underfoot. Case in point: when my daughter Jody was five years old, I was hauling the vacuum cleaner up the stairs, and she turned to me and said, "Grandma coming?"

But we forget that we didn't know our mothers when they first started housekeeping. By the time we began to notice, they'd already honed their skills and developed systems for getting things done. If I could change anything over the years, I would have worried less about the house. Hospitality is about people, not the surroundings. Happily, though, when I got busy writing, I could afford a little help around the house. And it's made it much easier for me to offer hospitality.

Staying connected is one of the hardest things to do. Friendship demands effort. I'm guessing that every one of us leads a busy life—it isn't just me. It may be that I travel more than some, but all of us pack our lives full of activities, work, chores, and expectations.

## The Hospitality-Challenged

Our childhoods have a lot to do with our hospitality comfort level. Some of us grew up in a welcoming home, while other families prized their privacy. A friend's mother used to say, "No kids in and no kids out." She loved having long stretches with just their nuclear family. So how do you find a happy medium if you are an entertainer married to someone who loves the quiet cocoon of his home?

For many years that was our situation. Wayne isn't as open to hospitality as I am because his background is much different than mine. But he's been willing to stretch. When we moved to Florida for part of each year, Wayne realized we had to be intentional about finding and growing friends who share our interests. So when we meet couples we enjoy, we understand it's going to take a commitment to keep growing the friendship. I recently received an e-mail from one couple we have not seen in a year. We couldn't believe a whole year had passed. Rather than saying a vague "We must get together," I e-mailed her back and said, "Let's set a date right now." You need to nail it down, otherwise the opportunity fades. Time goes by too quickly.

## Efficient Hospitality

An elderly couple from my friend's church invited them for dinner after they'd attended services for a month or so. When they sat down for an old-fashioned Sunday dinner, my friend was intrigued. How did this couple host a table of twelve to a full sit-down dinner with ham, scalloped potatoes, salads, relishes, home-baked breads, and cobbler when they'd been at church all morning? When my friend mentioned it later to one of the pastors who'd also been a guest, he laughed and told her the secret. Apparently they'd been doing this for years and had it down to a science. They use the same menu for every season. They make use of well-rehearsed to-do cards, and each one does his or her part to make the dinner happen. It's like clockwork, even down to the mix of guests they invite to the table—at least one pastor, one or two new families, some established families, singles, couples, young, old. By being systematic, this couple managed to entertain the entire church many times over. They welcomed strangers and helped people connect with one another.

## Radical Hospitality

St. Benedict, when he laid down his rules for hospitality, said, "Let all guests who arrive be received like Christ, for He is going to say, 'I came as a guest, and you received Me'" (see Matthew 25:35).

When I think of radical hospitality, I can't help thinking of the Quaker families who risked their lives and livelihood to shelter slaves through the Underground Railroad. Levi Coffin is perhaps the most well known. His house in Fountain City, Indiana, became known as Grand Central Station. "Seldom a week passed without our receiving passengers by this mysterious road," Coffin wrote. "We found it necessary to be always prepared to receive such company and properly care for them."[1]

Prepared to receive company and properly care for them. That meant hiding the "company" in a secret compartment of their wagon while transporting them to their next stop. It meant trying to throw off the scent of bloodhounds searching for fugitive slaves. The Coffins even sheltered Eliza Harris on her way to freedom. Eliza was made famous by Harriet Beecher Stowe's book *Uncle Tom's Cabin*.

Harriet Tubman also escaped slavery on the Underground Railroad, experiencing the hospitality of strangers all the way from Maryland to freedom. Rather than bask in her newfound freedom, she became the most famous "conductor" on that imaginary railroad. She went back to the plantations time after time and led more than three hundred other slaves to freedom. What a picture of the ripple effect of generosity.

In Harriet Tubman's life, that generosity and hospitality she received at the hands of strangers was multiplied thousands of times over. When the Civil War ended, she managed to buy a large home in Auburn, New York, where she cared for the homeless and the hungry. In her last years she grew vegetables and sold them door to door in order to raise the money to feed all who came to her home. Upon her death she left her house and her ministry to the church.

We may not be called to offer the kind of radical hospitality Levi Coffin and the Quakers offered or the selfless hospitality practiced by Harriet Tubman, but we often have the opportunity to open our homes and our hearts to strangers. In Hebrews 13:2 we're told, "Do not forget to entertain strangers, for by so doing some people have entertained angels without knowing it."

Angels. Just think!

## *Discovery*

*Whether we entertain friends or strangers,*
*we're told that the Lord is in our midst.*
*What company to keep.*

## SIMPLE ACTS OF HOSPITALITY

Developing your generosity in hospitality is far easier than you may think. Here are some tips for making hospitality work for you:

❖ Don't stress about your house. People count, not the state of your house. If it's too hard to get the house ready for company, use the yard.

❖ Work on developing several company menus. Use tried-and-true recipes. Write them on large index cards. On the back write the guests' names and the date you entertained them, so you can choose a different menu the next time.

❖ Create a shopping list and a to-do list for each menu card and attach them together. Entertaining is much easier when we don't stress about potentially forgetting something.

❖ Be creative about the places you can entertain. Your porch might be a wonderful setting for a supper party. A decorated garage might work perfectly for a child's birthday party.

❖ Let guests help with food. The nice thing about potlucks is that everyone invests in the gathering.

❖ Try to put interesting people together. Be generous about sharing your friends.

✤ Mix it up. Don't be afraid to mix age groups, couples and singles, church friends and neighborhood people.

✤ Figure out a style that works for you. Sometimes the simpler the event, the more successful it is.

**Praise be to the God and
Father of our Lord Jesus Christ,
the Father of compassion
and the God of all comfort,
who comforts us in all our troubles,
so that we can comfort those in any trouble
with the comfort we ourselves
have received from God.**

*2 Corinthians 1:3–4*

# Ten

# Waiting Rooms, Blossoms, and Letters That Last

## The Privilege of Inspiring Hope

I love the poem "Hope," by Emily Dickinson:

> "Hope" is the thing with feathers—
> That perches in the soul—
> And sings the tune without the words—
> And never stops—at all—
>
> And sweetest—in the Gale—is heard—
> And sore must be the storm—
> That could abash the little Bird
> That kept so many warm—

I've heard it in the chillest land—
And on the strangest Sea—
Yet—never—in Extremity,
It asked a crumb—of me.


My husband's best friend, Norm Frelinger, fell off the roof of his home. Norm is a do-it-yourself kind of guy. Strong and able. He'd been on that roof many times.

I'll never forget the look on Wayne's face when Norm's wife, Sharon, called from the hospital. "Norm broke every rib in his body and crushed three vertebrae. This is going to be a long recovery." Wayne and I spent many hours in the hospital with the Frelingers.

For a time Norm seemed to be recovering well. He was about to be released from the hospital when word came that a blood infection had taken hold and the outlook was grim. We were stunned to get the call that the doctors didn't expect him to last the night.

Norm and Sharon didn't have a church home, so I called our pastor and asked if he would go and pray with the family because it didn't look like Norm would survive much longer. Our senior pastor was gone—it was his day off—but our assistant pastor, Joel Morris, was available. Joel assured me he'd be happy to sit with Norm's family. He immediately left for the hospital and headed straight to the ICU waiting room. It only took him a moment to spot the grieving relatives. He walked up to them, greeted them, then sat with them for a time of conversation, prayer, and comfort. Over the course of the next hour he shared Scripture and the hope of eternal life through our Lord Jesus. They thanked him over and over. With one final prayer for strength, he left.

Our senior pastor called me the next day to find out about the situation with Norm and his family. When I told him that Norm had survived the night, he went to the hospital to visit the family again. Except there was no "again" to it. Norm's family had not seen Joel nor prayed with him the day before.

Joel had ministered to the *wrong* family.

The next Sunday, a sheepish-looking Joel came up to me and started to apologize. I stopped him. "No, Joel," I said, "God sent you specifically for that family." Joel had prayed with the very family who needed him most. Our friend Norm survived the night, and eventually the entire ordeal, but the mother of the family Joel prayed with didn't. There was no mistake at all—God knew. And He used the presence of a willing servant—a young pastor who was generous with his time and words of comfort—to make a huge difference, perhaps even an *eternal* difference, in the lives of a hurting family. It was one simple act.

"But I'm not a pastor," you might say. "I don't feel comfortable visiting people in hospitals, especially those facing life-threatening situations." I don't either. In fact, I can't think of many people who are at ease in those kinds of situations.

Dispensing hope doesn't always have to be awkward or difficult. Sometimes hope can be as simple as an encouraging word to a student who's failed a difficult test, or reassuring a young wife that the marriage isn't over after one bitter argument.

## Hope-filled Visits

In 1750 Samuel Johnson wrote, "Hope is necessary in every condition. The miseries of poverty, of sickness, of captivity, would, without this comfort, be insupportable." I discovered the need for dispensing hope when my cousin David fell ill. He was more like a brother than a cousin to me. We grew up together, not only as playmates, but we attended school and church together as well. When he was a young husband and father he was diagnosed with leukemia. That diagnosis rocked my world, but I was a new Christian, filled with optimistic assurance. I believed God would heal David. I didn't have a mustard-seed faith; this was at least avocado size.

When David was admitted to Fred Hutchinson Cancer Research Center, I spent time with him every day. Because I had faith that the cancer would miraculously disappear, I couldn't bring myself to talk with him about death, even when he broached the subject. It was as if, by denying it, I could stave off the inevitable. Instead, I talked about when we'd be riding motorcycles and taking long hikes. I reassured him it was only a matter of time before he walked out of that hospital, healthy and whole.

With more years under my belt, I now look back and wish I had given him the gift of understanding and listening, despite the pain that came with that reality. But even though I offered him my cockeyed optimism, he knew me well enough to recognize that my hopefulness was genuine and I truly believed he'd be healthy again. Hope perched in my very soul, and I know that when I shared my hope it took wing and lightened his heart in his final days.

As I've grown in my faith and caught a bit more of an eternal viewpoint, I've come to realize that my faith in his healing was not misplaced. David was, indeed, healed. Just not the way I had anticipated. When he entered heaven, he was exactly as I had pictured him—healthy, whole, and happy.

### Discovery

*We don't need to be professionally or theologically trained to offer hope and encouragement. We just need to be present.*

## Letters That Last

My friend tells the story of her aunt Emma who spent her high school years in bed. Born with progressive heart disease, she was only a teenager when she lay dying. In the last week of her life, Emma received a simple letter from an elderly family friend. It said:

*My dear Emma,*
*Good morning. I'm coming to make you a little call on paper*
*this morning. I want to show you this pretty flower that has*
*bloomed in my kitchen window for the last couple of weeks for*
*my inspiration and pleasure. It is the little plant from the slip*
*you gave me. Now I wanted you to see it. I hope you are not*
*suffering with too severe pain. "Let not your heart be troubled;*
*believe in God, believe also in me. In my Father's house are*
*many mansions" John 14.*

Tucked inside the letter were a pressed flower and a printed verse on a colored piece of cardstock: "Everlasting joy shall be upon their head: they shall obtain gladness and joy; and sorrow and mourning shall flee away. Isaiah 51, verse 11."

It's been decades since Emma died, but that letter had been saved. My friend's mother remembers Emma reading and rereading that letter in the days before she went home to be with the Lord. Though only about one hundred words, and written with less than perfect grammar, it is a letter filled with the promise of eternity.

You see, sometimes it only takes a letter. To dispense hope, we don't always have to go to the hospital every day the way I did with David. We simply need to be present in any way we can, even a visit on paper.

You've heard it said that the art of letter writing died with the advent of the telephone, e-mail, and text messages, but don't believe it. Nothing replaces the letter of encouragement, of comfort, or of condolence. Letters can be our lifeline to faraway friends and family, but don't overlook them for those suffering nearby. Although a visit offers time to listen, to laugh and cry together, a letter is tangible. It can be read when no one is around, or reread when fears threaten.

Letters of comfort and hope are often the hardest to write. It's so much easier to buy a commercial greeting card, simply signing our name to professionally produced sentiments.

The Lord invites us to comfort others with His comfort. And we know His comfort is never one size fits all. Our letter should strive to communicate the same love, the kind that grows out of relationship. But how do we do it? What do we say? What if we say the wrong thing? Emma's simple letter, written more than sixty years ago, holds the clues.

## *The True Source of Hope*

Inspired words emerge from time spent with the Lord. By spending time in prayer and the Word, we invite the Holy Spirit to join with us in gathering words of comfort and hope. Emma's letter goes on to say, "I think of you every day and ask God to help you." Perhaps it was because of time spent in prayer that this short message contained words that touched a chord in the young girl, filling her with hope.

I'm a much-published author, but no matter how much practice I've had composing words, I still approach the task of writing a difficult letter with a feeling of inadequacy. How can I know what will comfort or what may sound too smug or easy? Truth is, I can't. All I can do is leave my ineptitude in the Lord's hands and offer my shortcomings and my willingness to God and ask Him to fill in the blanks. So whether you are writing a letter, making a call, or visiting a suffering friend, if you would like to become a hope-bearer in the lives of hurting people, here are a few practical tips I have found to be helpful.

### Strive for Genuine Substance

General sentiments can be meaningless jargon. If we sense that a quick, cheerful note is best, then that is what we should do, but when it is time to offer real hope, we need to dig into a study of God's Word. There is nothing we are going through that Christ has not experienced—the Bible is relevant to every situation. Jesus wept with Lazarus' family on hearing of the death of his friend. Even though He knew this death was only temporary, Jesus was overcome with emotion. The more time we spend in the Bible, the more we come to understand the eternal nature of man— that death is just the beginning. Nothing helps us offer the gift of hope more than understanding why there is hope. When you visit or write a note to a special friend, make sure you mention what that friendship has meant and the ways in which your friend has touched your life. We all need to know that we've connected and have made a difference. What a perfect time to deliver that message to your hurting friend.

### Resist the Tendency to Offer Answers

This is not the time to try to "make sense" of suffering. There are no pat answers. We humans have long struggled with the why of it. It is far better to talk about our feelings and to concentrate on the One Who is the Answer. Don't be afraid of silence. Sometimes just sitting with a friend is enough.

When I lost my father and then, a short year later, my mother, the letters I received offered a lifeline. Our friends reaffirmed their love for us. We could read between the lines and see the sentiments they struggled to express. Even the discomfort we sometimes sensed in their attempt to find the right words was honest and heartening. There were no right words, only loving letters, but it was enough. Their words were arms of love and comfort that surrounded me and my family.

## Focus on Life and Hope

No matter how desperate the situation, there is always hope. Even if physical healing is not likely, we can find eternal hope and eternal healing in the life, death, and resurrection of Jesus Christ. As C. S. Lewis said to a friend, "Christians never say good-bye."

There is hope in each new day. The letter written to Emma included a pressed flower snipped off the plant propagated from her cutting. What a symbol of regeneration! No words are needed. Simple statements like "The dawn sky was streaked with color as I walked to the gate this morning" remind us that the world is God's and the sun rises each day. Hope springs from such reminders.

One of the most surprising things for me as an author has been the number of letters that I receive. Oftentimes I'll get letters from people who are in a lot of emotional pain. They write to thank me and to tell me that my stories helped them escape after long periods of time in a hospital waiting room. My books were there just when they needed them.

Such letters have made me realize that God gave me this gift of storytelling to help others through painful times. When their letters come, they touch my heart. I can't just ignore that. I can't just say, "What a wonderful letter," and set it aside. And so over the years I've gotten in the habit of sending back a card with a few words of encouragement and hope. I've been able to identify with so many of my readers. If they tell me that they've lost their mother or father, I know the pain of losing a parent. I know what that's like to feel lost and empty and alone.

I give them a Bible verse. And then I add a pamphlet on how to get through grief with God's help. Or my correspondent may be someone who has a sick husband or someone who has cancer. There are pamphlets that I've been able to get through the Guideposts Foundation that address these issues and offer hope and encouragement.

### Recall Memories and Shared Experiences

Have you ever noticed how people love to laugh and share stories at funerals? You know why, don't you? Stories connect us in a deep, personal way. "I'll never forget the time" often ushers in a long-forgotten memory. Knowing that someone is critically ill makes friendship, kinship, and shared experiences all the more precious to us. Don't be afraid to say that. And don't be afraid to spin stories. "I remember when" stories are always welcome, especially the humorous ones. Nothing lightens the load like laughter and recalling happy times.

When it became evident that my cousin David wasn't going to survive, his father, my uncle Bernard, and I sat in the hospital waiting area exchanging memories of David. I'd grown up with my cousin and never noticed that he had a third nipple until I sat by him there in the hospital. I mentioned that to my uncle, who calmly looked at me and said, "I don't know how David got so lucky. I could have used that extra nipple myself." With that we both burst into gales of laughter. It was the release we needed from the grief that crowded our hearts. It broke the terrible tension that threatened to overwhelm us.

### Don't Be Afraid to Address the Real Battle

Share in the suffering. This is the hardest part for me. I find it much easier to laugh or to encourage. But when the time comes to cry together, my natural instinct is to try to make everything better. When we're writing letters of hope and comfort, we shouldn't omit the words that let our friend know that we are suffering as well.

In Emma's letter, near the end, her friend awkwardly comments about her pain and then in a stream-of-consciousness passage, goes on to offer the hope of many mansions. There's something genuine that comes through those words. The pain for Emma is temporary and all glory awaits her. Jesus is waiting on the other side, and He's prepared a special place just for her where she will be free of pain and will never be ill again.

### Be Willing to Face Eternity

Share in the comfort. This is where faith makes a difference. The much-loved Bible verse John 3:16 tells us, "For God so loved the world that he gave his one and only Son, that whoever believes in him shall not perish but have eternal life." It couldn't be much clearer than that, could it? Whoever believes in Jesus, God's son, is going to live forever. Even when a friend is dying, we know he is only crossing over into real living—eternal living. It is much like C. S. Lewis writes at the close of *The Last Battle,* the final book in *The Chronicles of Narnia,* when the children in the story realize they have died and left the Shadowlands: "The term is over: the holidays have begun. The dream is ended: this is the morning."[1]

Our perspective determines how we understand death. From an earthly perspective we see loss, but from the eternal perspec-

tive, entering heaven is triumph. The Bible verse from Isaiah
that came in Emma's letter offered that eternal view: " . . . they
shall obtain gladness and joy; and sorrow and mourning shall flee
away" (Isaiah 51:11; King James Version).

When we are at a loss for words, there is nothing better than
using those of the Great Comforter. The passages of comfort in the
Bible are so vivid, they offer a cooling balm. Your search for those
verses will comfort you as well.

There is no time that our words are more precious than when
we offer them to comfort a friend. God, the father of all comfort,
invites us to draw on His comfort and to share it with others.

## *Discovery*

*Hope is not a gift we have to manufacture ourselves.*
*It is a gift from the God Who delights in giving the best to His children.*
*All we need do to give this gift is invite others to join us*
*in looking to the Giver.*

## SIMPLE ACTS OF HOPE

✤ Keep a box of note cards or stationery in a convenient
location, along with a book of stamps and a pen. So often,
we intend to send cards but don't get around to it. I know
a family who keeps theirs in a box in the dining room. Over
dinner they often share news about friends and family. How
convenient to write a card then and pass it around the table
for everyone to sign.

*(Continued)*

◈ The Bible is filled with passages of hope and consolation. Here are a few of my favorites. You'll want to take time to search for others, since much of the hope we offer will come from the time spent in God's Word.

"I am the Lord, the God of all mankind. Is anything too hard for me?" (Jeremiah 32:27)

"'Though the mountains be shaken and the hills be removed, yet my unfailing love for you will not be shaken nor my covenant of peace be removed,' says the Lord, who has compassion on you." (Isaiah 54:10)

"Listen to me . . . you whom I have upheld since you were conceived, and have carried since your birth. Even to your old age and gray hairs I am he, I am he who will sustain you. I have made you and I will carry you; I will sustain you and I will rescue you." (Isaiah 46:3–4)

"For I am convinced that neither death nor life, neither angels nor demons, neither the present nor the future, nor any powers, neither height nor depth, nor anything else in all creation, will be able to separate us from the love of God that is in Christ Jesus our Lord." (Romans 8:38–39)

"Praise be to the Lord, to God our Savior, who daily bears our burdens. Our God is a God who saves; from the Sovereign Lord comes escape from death." (Psalm 68:19–20)

"Fear not, for I have redeemed you; I have summoned you by name; you are mine. When you pass through the waters, I will be with you; and when you pass through the rivers, they will not sweep over you. When you walk through the fire, you will not be burned; the flames will not set you ablaze." (Isaiah 43:1–2)

"Cast all your anxiety on him because he cares for you." (1 Peter 5:7)

"The Lord is the everlasting God, the Creator of the ends of the earth. He will not grow tired or weary, and his understanding no one can fathom. He gives strength to the weary and increases the power of the weak. Even youths grow tired and weary, and young men stumble and fall; but those who hope in the Lord will renew their strength. They will soar on wings like eagles; they will run and not grow weary, they will walk and not be faint." (Isaiah 40:28–31)

The Word became flesh and made

his dwelling among us.

We have seen his glory,

the glory of the One and Only

who came from the Father,

full of grace and truth.

John 1:14

## Eleven

# Glue, Legends, and a Slumber Party

## The Spirit of Christmas

Everyone who knows me knows I love Christmas. Maybe it's the child in me or maybe it's because it's the one season of the year when generosity is a national pastime—I don't know. All I know is, it's the celebration of my Savior's birthday, and I can't think of a more wonderful time of year.

### The Glue That Holds Us Together

Because we focus on the spiritual meaning of Christmas, I love to decorate with nativity scenes. Confession: we have nativity scenes in every room of our home. I joke that you can't even go to the bathroom in our house without baby Jesus watching your every move. I especially love the huge Italian nativity that I set up in my library. The figures are probably three or four feet high.

Even though I love Christmas, not every Christmas has been easy in the Macomber household. And one particular Christmas-time was an especially troublesome season. It was the first Christmas without my mom. One of my closest cousins had just been diagnosed with breast cancer. And, if that wasn't enough, a dear friend had also received a cancer diagnosis. It was hard to be merry.

It was Christmas Eve, and after a busy day with kids and grand-kids, I finally headed to bed. Turning out the lights one by one, I stepped into the library. There in the manger lay baby Jesus with his arm broken off. With my feet rooted to the floor, I stood there looking at Him. I felt broken too. All those troubles seemed to come bearing down. You know how it is.

I must have said something out loud because Wayne came in and put an arm around me. "Oh, honey," he said and left the rest unsaid. He walked out of the room and returned a moment later with a special adhesive. Within a couple of minutes he had glued the arm back on baby Jesus. My husband's actions were a simple act of kindness and love. But it shook me out of myself. Seeing that mended arm reminded me that Jesus is the glue that holds us all together. And, you know, it was a wonderful Christmas despite it being the first without Mom and the worries over my cousin and dear friend. We experienced the glue of God's love.

I can't help myself. I treasure that nativity even more now with the repair. I decorate six Christmas trees each year and festoon nearly every bush and tree outside with twinkling lights. We deck the halls with great enthusiasm. Oh I love Christmas. When a guest steps into my house she can't help but know and recognize immediately that we celebrate the real reason for the season—Jesus.

Remember when I said that giving aligns us with the heart of God? I think that's why people are more attuned to spiritual mat-ters at Christmas. That giving spirit sensitizes so many people to the

Giver of all gifts, even if they don't realize it. So for that reason, I've found that Christmas is the perfect time to gather friends together. I host two Christmas teas, sometimes three, to which I invite groups of friends who share a common interest. My house helps tell the story of our faith at that time of year and is a great conversation starter.

## Gift Giving

We can't address discovering the power of generosity at Christmas without talking about gifts. As the holidays roll around and cash registers ring, it's easy to succumb to the bah, humbug spirit. You might wonder why we give gifts at Christmas anyway. Some people point to St. Nicholas, the inspiration for our modern Santa Claus. Nicholas lived during the third and fourth centuries in a small village in what. is now Turkey. He grew up in a wealthy family, but both parents died in an epidemic when he young. Nicholas's deep faith led him to take Jesus's words to heart. He set out to sell what he owned and to give the money to the poor. Nicholas spent the rest of his life giving his fortune away. He cared for widows, orphans, those without dowries, the sick, the suffering, sailors, and children. His life work was giving.

Others point to the story of the Magi. "When they saw the star, they were overjoyed. On coming to the house, they saw the child with his mother Mary, and they bowed down and worshiped him. Then they opened their treasures and presented him with gifts of gold and of incense and of myrrh" (Matthew 2:10–11). The wise men traveled from distant lands, following the miraculous star, and when they finally found Jesus, they not only worshiped him, they brought gifts.

## The Greatest Gift of All

But, of course, the greatest gift of all was given at Christmas. God gave His Son Jesus. "For God so loved the world that he gave his one and only Son, that whoever believes in him shall not perish but have eternal life" (John 3:16). When I give gifts at Christmas, it is remembering the greatest gift of all, the birth that changed the world forever. In Philippians 2:6–8 we see God's plan from birth to death: "Who, being in very nature God, did not consider equality with God something to be grasped, but made himself nothing, taking the very nature of a servant, being made in human likeness. And being found in appearance as a man, he humbled himself and became obedient to death—even death on a cross!"

It's such a miracle. The God of the universe Who cannot be contained, the God Who created all, comes to earth to save humankind and allows Himself to be contained in a womb for nine months—we just can't seem to wrap our understanding around it. And so as we celebrate the gift of God's Son we give gifts to one another. We slow down the frenetic pace of our lives and we remember. We celebrate this mystery beyond our understanding.

## Legendary Giving

I love the Christmas legends that address the idea of giving gifts at Christmas. One of my favorites is the legend of the poinsettia. The story goes that in a small Mexican village it was the custom for children to bring gifts to the Christ child of the crèche on Christmas morning. The children spent days deciding what to bring. One boy found a dove and put it in a basket. Another dug up a little piece of metal that looked like gold in a certain light. One of the girls made a beautiful clay pot. The children could talk about little else.

Maria had nothing to bring. Her family was the poorest in the village, but she longed to bring a gift to Jesus. As the children began entering the church with their gifts, she gathered a bundle of dry sticks and wrapped them in a bit of cloth. One by the one, the children brought their beautiful gifts toward the altar. As the dove flew out of the basket and perched on the wing of an angel, Maria felt ashamed. She looked at her bundle of dry sticks and stood to leave the church. How could she have thought to bring such a worthless gift to the baby Jesus?

She looked toward the crèche one last time and felt strangely drawn toward it. Stepping out into the aisle, she heard the other children gasp. She looked down at the bundle of sticks, and as she moved toward the altar, she watched each dry stick burst into a blood-red bloom—the most beautiful flower any of the villagers had ever seen.

According to the legend, it was her one simple act, her willingness to bring what she had—her own little loaves and fishes, so to speak—that led to the very first Christmas poinsettia.

## Gifts from the Heart

I work hard to make sure that the job of buying and giving gifts doesn't upstage the true meaning of Christmas. Several years ago, one of the ladies in my swimming group told us about how she got together with her cousins every year at Christmas for a slumber party. I loved the idea.

It was a time of transition for our family. My two daughters and daughters-in-law had all started housekeeping. Several babies had come into the family or were on their way. I couldn't stop thinking about how fun it would be to have a giant slumber party with all of the kids and grandkids at my house. We could stay up all night. Of course, if we were to stay awake until morning, we had to find things to do. So I made a list of all the ways to fill the time. The girls threw in their ideas, and we decided it would be the perfect opportunity to make homemade gifts for others.

Jennifer found a book series called Gifts in a Bag.[1] One book features dips you could make and individually package, another book has recipes for meat rubs and seasonings, and another book has recipes for wonderful drink mixes. We decided what items we would make that first slumber party and made lists of ingredients so we could shop ahead of time. Then my daughter Jennifer, who has this great organizational mind, came up with the idea of setting up stations, and our family—grandparents, kids, grandkids—became one huge assembly line for making our own Christmas gifts.

It has become a Macomber tradition. When we have our slumber party the house smells of cider, spices, and chocolate. And the sounds of laughter fill every corner. Little hands spill ingredients, and as much goes into the mouths as into the bags, but no one cares. We make enough gifts for everyone's teachers, mailmen, pastors, friends, and others. I love that our family focuses on giving, but even more precious is the time we spend together. I'm guessing that our grandchildren will never smell mulling spices or cocoa without remembering those long, wonderful nights.

## Gifts with Eternal Value

A few weeks ago, Amanda W., one of my readers, wrote: "For the past fourteen years I have given my husband the same Christmas present, the gift of service. I write him a letter and tell him what I am going to do in his honor over the next year. The project always has something to do with who we are and what is going on in our lives. The first year I made personal hygiene bags for women in shelters. I told him it was because I was thankful I'm married to a man who is so good to me and treats me like a queen. I wanted the women in crisis to know that even though they were in a bad situation, someone cared. It wasn't huge but it was what I could do at that time."

Her letter continued, "One year I found out about a lady who had three foster daughters who all had AIDS. She had just found out that she had breast cancer but wanted to keep the girls so that they would feel safe. I made bags or baskets for every holiday that year for each of the girls so this wonderful woman would have one less thing to worry about.

"I have done lots of different things over the years. I've repeated some of the things for several years in a row in addition to whatever new adventure I come up with. I don't want you to think I am trying to brag about what I have done. Only those who are really close to me know that I do this for my husband for Christmas."

Amanda needn't worry that I would think she was bragging. I think she is doing exactly what the Lord calls each of us to do when He called us to live in a spirit of generosity. She took her own resources, decided on one simple act, and found others to bless. What a gift for her husband that was multiplied over and over. That is the spirit of Christmas.

## Reunions at Christmas

I think about families like ours gathering together at Christmas. It's one of my favorite things about the season. Every time I hear a story of a Christmas reunion, it just melts my heart. My friend's pastor told this story to his congregation last Christmas. I've tried to track down the provenance of the story but it's been told and retold so many times, the origin seems to have been lost in the retelling. Some say it was originally written by a man named Howard C. Schade. Whether the account is true or not, we never tire of hearing stories of unforgettable reunions at Christmas.

*In the autumn of 1954 a young pastor and his wife moved to Brooklyn to take his first church assignment. Instead of coming to a thriving congregation, he had nothing but a dilapidated church building that had been closed for a long time. He didn't mind but jumped into the work, setting Christmas Eve as his goal for reopening the neighborhood church. He and his wife cleaned floors, plastered walls, sanded and stained pews, and painted until late every night. The work was grueling but their enthusiasm made the hours pass quickly. Christmas was approaching and they finished four days early.*

*That night, as they locked the building, it started to sprinkle. Over the next two days the rain never let up. The pastor kept looking out at the trees bending in the torrential downpour, wondering if the slate on the roof would hold.*

*As soon as the storm abated he walked over to the church, praying that there'd be no damage. When he unlocked the door, the sag of his shoulders revealed his discouragement. With one glance he could see that, just as he feared, the roof had leaked. Water had run down the wall behind the pulpit, softening the new plaster enough so that huge chunks of plaster and lath had fallen off the wall onto the floor. He got the broom and dustpan and managed to clean up the sodden mess, but there was nothing that could be done about the gaping hole above the pulpit. There couldn't have been a worse place for this to happen than right over the altar. Should they postpone the first service? He hated the idea of missing the celebration of the Lord's birth, especially since they'd been inviting people from all over the Brooklyn neighborhood.*

*On his way home he stepped inside the secondhand store, thinking he may as well remove the handbill announcing the service from the window. Spread across a table, however, an ivory crocheted tablecloth caught his eye. In the center was a cross, crocheted in a delicate fillet stitch. As he lifted a corner, he could tell it was big enough to cover the entire missing patch of plaster in the church. Without hesitation, he* bought the tablecloth. The owner folded it and wrapped it in brown paper tied with twine.

As the pastor walked back toward the church he watched an elderly woman dart from a doorway toward a bus pulling away from the curb. "It looks like you've missed the bus," he said. "The next one won't be along for forty-five minutes."

The woman pulled her coat around her.

"I'm just going over to the church to do one last thing before our Christmas Eve service. It's nice and warm in there. Would you like to come wait inside?"

The woman mumbled a shy thanks and followed him, slipping into the last pew.

The pastor got out the ladder and his hammer, nailing a line of brads evenly along the wall above the hole in the plaster. He gingerly placed the tablecloth over the nails, easing them through the openwork of the crochet. He forgot all about the woman until she spoke.

"Sir," she said in a hushed voice, "where did you get that tablecloth?"

He told her, pointing toward the secondhand store.

"Look in the lower right-hand corner," she said as she moved toward the front. "Are the initials EBG worked into the border?"

He came down off the ladder and looked. Sure enough, there were the initials. "How did you know?"

"I made that tablecloth thirty-five years ago in Austria. See how large it is? We had a table that held our entire family—parents, uncles, aunts, children." She wiped a hand across her cheek. "Gone. All gone."

"Gone?" The pastor didn't understand.

"When the Nazis came, my husband told me to leave. There was no time to take anything. He was to follow me a week later, but I was captured by the SS and taken to a camp."

"Taken to a camp?" The pastor sat down.

"I never saw any of them again."

"Let me get the tablecloth down for you," he said, moving toward the ladder.

"No. No. You keep it. Look at how beautiful it is here in the dim light of your church."

The woman was right. The tablecloth added texture and design to the wall. It was much more interesting than the smooth plaster had been. He knew it would be even more beautiful in candlelight. "Let me go home and get my car. My wife and I will drive you home."

The woman agreed. She lived in Staten Island and had come to Brooklyn only to clean a house that day. The pastor kept thinking about how unlikely it was that she'd have been in their church on that very day to see her own handiwork from a life long gone. Coincidence? Both he and his wife just kept shaking their heads.

Christmas Eve dawned cold and clear. By evening snowflakes had begun to swirl, but the pastor was delighted to see the little church nearly full. The scent of candles, the sound of bells, and the strains of ancient carols filled the sanctuary.

After the service, people filed out into the night. The pastor noticed an old man still sitting in the pew. He'd seen him in the neighborhood, always alone. The pastor sat down beside him, thinking he needed a kind word or two on this lonely night.

"That tablecloth," the man said, pointing a shaking finger toward the altar. "My wife made that tablecloth. I can still remember her working on it during the long winter nights in Austria."

"Your wife?" The pastor sat stunned.

"Yes. She fled Austria just before the occupation. I was to follow, but I was arrested and taken to prison." The man put his head in his hands and wept. "I never saw her again."

The pastor motioned to his wife to come over. "We're going for a ride." He turned toward the man. "I have someone I'd like you to meet."

The man seemed happy for the diversion. They drove in silence, watching the snow dance in the headlights. *When they arrived at the woman's apartment building, they helped the man walk up the three flights to the woman's apartment. They knocked on the door. As it opened, they saw a reunion the likes of which they knew they would never see again.*

## *Discovery*

*The perfect gift at Christmas has already been given—the Son of God. The best act of generosity we can offer at Christmas is to celebrate this gift by spending time with our family, our friends, and the One Who was the greatest gift of all.*

## SIMPLE ACTS OF SHARING THE SPIRIT OF CHRISTMAS

So what makes a perfect gift given in the spirit of Christmas? The intent behind the gift is paramount. The Apostle Paul knew that the secret of giving lies in the heart. He said, "Each man should give what he has decided in his heart to give, not reluctantly or under compulsion, for God loves a cheerful giver" (2 Corinthians 9:7). If your gift reflects a duty or carries the expectation of reciprocity, it can't possible convey cheerfulness.

The ideal gift celebrates something shared. Here are some gift ideas that might spark further creativity:

(Continued)

### The Gift That Opens Possibilities

✧ Has your friend always wanted to learn to knit? Consider a gift certificate for a class at your local knit shop. Even better, how about a class you can attend together?

✧ An unexpected gift opens a world of possibilities—like a set of watercolors, one or two brushes, and watercolor paper for an artistic family member.

### The Gift That Says You Are Listening

✧ Listen to your friends and family. If you hear them longing for a day or two away, offer the gift of childcare as a present.

✧ Has an elderly friend worried about all the fix-it jobs that need doing? What about providing a handyman for an afternoon?

### The Gift That Promises

✧ Nothing is more romantic than a gift offering a promise. Instead of a dozen roses, why not a single rose on your first Christmas together, two on your second, and so on? When you give a bouquet of fifty roses on your golden Christmas you see what a promise fulfilled looks like.

✧ On the day our friends adopted their oldest daughter, they gave her a tiny gold cross. At the end of that day they put it away to give to her again on her wedding day as a reminder of God's hand on her life throughout her childhood.

### The Gift That Encourages Growth

❖ What about a devotional book, some sharp pencils tied with raffia, and a blank journal? It is a gentle way to encourage growth through devotional time.

❖ For your teens, check out the excellent personal growth workbooks that are available at your Christian bookseller. These combine the discovery about self with the study of God's Word.

> *I was hungry and you gave me something to eat, I was thirsty and you gave me something to drink, I was a stranger and you invited me in.*
>
> Matthew 25:35

# Twelve

# *Bread Crumbs, Minnows, and Submarines*

## *The Gift of Caregiving*

My swimming friend, Jesse, is in his eighties. He fought in World War II and was part of the French Resistance. I bonded with Jessie from the very beginning because my dad was in France in World War II, though Dad was captured by the Germans in the Battle of the Bulge and spent the rest of the war in a German concentration camp. But Jesse and my dad were kindred spirits.

Jesse loved his wife, Dovie—loved her deeply. She suffered from Alzheimer's disease, but it made no difference to Jesse. He was devoted to her. He took care of her for many years. When he could no longer physically care for her, he arranged for her to stay in a care facility.

It didn't matter that he no longer had the sole job of taking care of her; Jesse went to the care facility to spend each day with her. He fed her, bathed her, and cared for her physical needs, day in and day out.

Dovie eventually died, but Jesse continues to stop by the care facility every day to help care for the other residents he's come to know. I have a feeling I know what the Lord thinks of Jesse's work.

## God's Directive

We hear many warm stories of selfless caregiving, but the truth is, it can be a tough, scary task. We know God calls us to care for others, but the reality is so . . . well, so daily. Sometimes it's messy. And sometimes our beloved patient doesn't know us or even becomes angry or stubborn when we are trying to help. It's not easy, but if we are seeking to live in a spirit of generosity, that spirit needs to extend to the helpless.

The Bible is far from silent about caregiving. If it's our parents who need the care, there's this commandment: "Honor your father and your mother, so that you may live long in the land the Lord your God is giving you" (Exodus 20:12). Most people think the verse pertains to young children obeying their parents—and it does—but read it again. It seems to me that honoring also means caring for them.

If you have any doubts, listen to the words of Paul: "Give proper recognition to those widows who are really in need. But if a widow has children or grandchildren, these should learn first of all to put their religion into practice by caring for their own family and so repaying their parents and grandparents, for this is pleasing to God. The widow who is really in need and left all alone puts her hope in God and continues night and day to pray and to ask God for help. But the widow who lives for pleasure is dead even while she lives. Give the people these instructions, too, so that no one may be open to blame. If anyone does not provide for his relatives, and especially for his immediate family, he has denied the faith and is worse than an unbeliever" (1 Timothy 5:3–8).

## The Second Voice

But caregiving is more than a mandate from God. There are hidden benefits inherent in it. I'll never forget the article I read in *Christianity Today* several years back. Philip Yancey wrote about the last years of Henri Nouwen's life. Nouwen was a psychologist, priest, and theologian. He taught at Notre Dame, Harvard, and Yale. He wrote more than a book a year and spoke all over the world. But in the last years of his life, Henri Nouwen gave it all up to become a caregiver to a profoundly disabled man. In part, here's what Philip Yancey wrote about his last visit with Henri Nouwen:

*After lunch we celebrated a special Eucharist for Adam, the young man Nouwen looked after. With solemnity, but also a twinkle in his eye, Nouwen led the liturgy in honor of Adam's twenty-sixth birthday. Unable to talk, walk, or dress himself, profoundly retarded, Adam gave no sign of comprehension. He seemed to recognize, at least, that his family had come. He drooled throughout the ceremony and grunted loudly a few times.*

*Later Nouwen told me it took him nearly two hours to prepare Adam each day. Bathing and shaving him, brushing his teeth, combing his hair, guiding his hand as he tried to eat breakfast—these* simple, repetitive acts had become for him almost like an hour of meditation.

I must admit I had a fleeting doubt as to whether this was the best use of the busy priest's time. Could not someone else take over the manual chores? When I cautiously broached the subject with Nouwen himself, he informed me that I had completely misinterpreted him. "I am not giving up anything," he insisted. "It is I, not Adam, who gets the main benefit from our friendship."

All day Nouwen kept circling back to my question, bringing up various ways he had benefitted from his relationship with Adam. It had been difficult for him at first, he said. Physical touch, affection, and the messiness of caring for an uncoordinated person did not come easily. But he had learned to love Adam, truly to love him. In the process he had learned what it must be like for God to love us— spiritually uncoordinated, retarded, able to respond with what must seem to God like inarticulate grunts and groans. Indeed, working with Adam had taught him the humility and "emptiness" achieved by desert monks only after much discipline.

Nouwen has said that all his life two voices competed inside him. One encouraged him to succeed and achieve, while the other called him simply to rest in the comfort that he was "the beloved" of God. Only in the last decade of his life did he truly listen to that second voice.[1]

## Ripple Effect

When we're in the middle of caregiving, it can be difficult to imagine any benefit to us. We may be tired, worried, and barely able to see beyond the next meal or doctor visit. But as Henri Nouwen discovered, through caregiving we can find the power of humility and the kind of silence that is filled with deeper things.

My friend's mother lived with her for many years. When her mother's health began to fail, my friend decided to continue to care for her at home with the help of hospice. It was work for which she'd never been prepared, but she insists she wouldn't trade the experience for anything. She said that keeping watch over the end of her mother's days made life all the more precious to her. And as her children helped her care for her mother, she was modeling how families care for one another. I'm guessing that when my friend's time comes to leave this earth, her children will care for her in the same way they saw her caring for her mother. We pass our values on to our children—it's that ripple effect.

When we stretch ourselves to do the tough stuff, we grow in ways we'd never imagined. We may feel impatience, despair, and even revulsion, but as we perform one simple act of obedience after another something begins to develop in us. When our job of caregiving is over, we will not be the same people. Yes, some caregivers will be left bitter and resentful, but if we seek to discover the blessings inherent in our service, we'll find that we are better than we were before—more tender, more patient, and more attuned to what Henri Nouwen called "the second voice."

## Facing the Task

I have read that everyone falls into one of four groups: those who have been caregivers, those who are caregivers, those who will be caregivers, and those who will need caregivers. It's not something we can ignore. In the last months of my mother's life she lived near us in Port Orchard at a care facility. I was able to care for her on a daily basis. I spent time with her and listened to her. Perhaps the most profound lesson I learned in those last months with my mother was patience. She would repeatedly tell me the same things. And I would give the same answer time after time. It required more patience than I thought imaginable, but as long as I listened, as long as I stayed with her, God granted me the resources I needed. It helped tremendously that my children were so good to her, especially my daughters. They visited regularly, even when Mom became so forgetful. At the end, she couldn't remember my daughters, Jody and Jennifer, but she could remember Jennifer's littlest one, Isaiah. Jennifer would faithfully bring Isaiah to visit. Mom loved being around this toddler great-grandson. Just loved it.

## Resources for Caregiving

We've talked a lot about loaves and fishes in this book. And of course by that I mean our resources. As I've said, we can only give back of what we've been given. When it comes to caregiving, sometimes we feel as if our resources are stretched paper thin. Forget loaves and fishes—sometimes we are left to ask if we even have a few bread crumbs to spare, or a minnow or two.

When we undertake a tough assignment, we need to be able to gather our forces. You might need to find an excellent care facility. Or if you decide to provide care at home, there are many agencies and organizations available to help caregivers. Locate them and use their services. Or you may quickly find yourself in need of respite care, medical supplies, meals, and even a sympathetic ear. Those services are available. An Internet search will uncover more resources than you ever thought existed.

Encourage your church to stand behind you. If they have a Stephen Ministry—that's a ministry that consists of trained laypeople who provide one-to-one Christian care to hurting people in and around your congregation—see if you can be assigned a Stephen minister to walk with you. If your church doesn't have experience supporting caregivers, do your best to educate them. Just as there are biblical mandates for us to care for family and widows, there are mandates for the church as well. You might just be the one to help your church learn how to walk alongside caregivers.

I am grateful to God that, even as a writer, I've been able to stand alongside caregivers in a way I would have never anticipated. I had this note from Vivian Furlong, one of my readers: "My husband and I have been caring for my parents during the past five years and your books have been my escape during many very tough times as we dealt with all the challenges of making their last years as good as possible and now going on without them. I know I will see them again in Heaven but am trying to figure out how to live without them in my world until that day comes. Thank you for keeping faith and family alive in today's fiction. God bless you always."

## Dealing with the Pressure

Naturally there is stress inherent in caring for the basic needs of someone who can no longer care for himself. I love the way Jay Kessler, president emeritus of Taylor University in Upland, Indiana, illustrated it:

*There are two ways of handling pressure. One is illustrated by a bathysphere, the miniature submarine used to explore the ocean in places so deep that the water pressure would crush a conventional submarine like an aluminum can. Bathyspheres compensate with plate steel several inches thick, which keeps the water out but also makes them heavy and hard to maneuver.*

*Inside they're not alone. When their lights are turned on and you look through the tiny, thick plate-glass windows, what do you see? Fish! These fish cope with extreme pressure in an entirely different way. They don't build thick skins; they remain supple and free. They compensate for the outside pressure through equal and opposite pressure inside themselves. Christians, likewise, don't have to be hard and thick-skinned—as long as they appropriate God's power within to equal the pressure without.*

We need to lean on God to keep us supple and free.

## When It's Time to Let Go

When you are nearing what you believe may be the end of a loved one's life, I suggest you contact your local hospice. They will help assess when the time is right for them to step in and assist. I have found these loving, generous volunteers to be wonderful. They've walked the path many times, and they walked alongside me when it was time for my mother to be with the Lord. These organizations offers everything needed to care for those we love and help them cross over.

The hardest thing about caregiving for me was when it was no longer needed. When our loved one goes to be with the Lord, only then do we realize how great is the loss. In chapter 10, we came to the conclusion that if we are going to be generous in dispensing hope, we must have an eternal perspective. One of the poems that has helped me most in this was written by the pastor and poet Henry van Dyke (1852–1933):

## GONE FROM MY SIGHT

I am standing upon the seashore.
A ship at my side spreads her white
sails to the morning breeze and starts
for the blue ocean.

She is an object of beauty and strength.
I stand and watch her until at length
she hangs like a speck of white cloud
just where the sea and sky come
to mingle with each other.

Then someone at my side says;
"There, she is gone!"

"Gone where?"

Gone from my sight. That is all.
She is just as large in mast and hull
and spar as she was when she left my side
and she is just as able to bear her
load of living freight to her destined port.

Her diminished size is in me, not in her.

And just at the moment when someone
at my side says: "There, she is gone!"
there are other eyes watching her coming,
and other voices ready to take up the glad shout;

"Here she comes!"
And that is dying.[2]

## TIPS FOR CAREGIVERS

### FROM THE NATIONAL
### FAMILY CAREGIVERS ASSOCIATION

Did you notice that I changed the name of this feature for this chapter on caregiving? I had to, of course, because the simple truth is that caregiving is *not* simple at all. The National Family Caregivers Association has compiled these helpful tips. Following them will help us persevere as we are generous in caregiving.

1. Caregiving is a job, and respite is your earned right. *Reward yourself* with respite breaks often.

2. *Watch out* for signs of depression and don't delay getting professional help when needed.

3. When others offer to help, *accept* and suggest specific ways in which they can assist.

4. *Educate yourself* about your loved one's condition and how to communicate effectively with doctors.

5. There's a difference between caring and doing. *Be open* to technologies and ideas that promote your loved one's independence.

6. *Trust your instincts.* Most of the time they'll lead you in the right direction.

7. Caregivers often do a lot of lifting, pushing, and pulling. *Be good to your back.*

8. Grieve for your losses, and then allow yourself to *dream new dreams.*

9. *Seek support* from other caregivers. There is great strength in knowing you are not alone.

10. *Stand up for your rights* as a caregiver and a citizen.[3]

*Let us not become weary of doing good,*

*for at the proper time we will reap a harvest*

*if we do not give up.*

*Therefore, as we have opportunity,*

*let us do good to all people.*

*Galatians 6:9–10*

## Thirteen

# A Kingdom, Ten Dollars, and Afghans of Love

### The Bounty of Time

Time.

I love what Norman Vincent Peale said, "The more you lose yourself in something bigger than yourself, the more energy you will have."

What a concept! Choosing to lose ourselves in the big things, the eternal things, will energize us. We already know that spending our lives as slaves to the mundane drains us and causes us to lose sight of the goal. But the opposite is true as well. Investing ourselves in the truly important things multiplies the value of our time.

In our society nothing is as scarce as gifts of time, and yes, this kind of generosity takes time that could be used for more "productive" activities, but nothing is so desperately needed as time spent on people.

We come back to our theme again. If we are to discover the deep power of generosity we need to be able to pursue the big things—the mission to which God has called us. We all have the same twenty-four hours a day. I've often wondered how it is that some people seem to move mountains while others barely make it over speed bumps.

First of all, we need to know what the big things are. If we don't prioritize, we will find ourselves doing the things that scream the loudest for our attention. You've heard the expression "Good is often the enemy of the best." We must figure out what God's best is for us. Fortunately, we don't have to search in agony over this discovery. Jesus spelled it out very clearly.

In Matthew 6:32–33, Jesus talks about our treasures. Here's what he said: "For the pagans run after all these things, and your heavenly Father knows that you need them. But seek first his kingdom and his righteousness, and all these things will be given to you as well."

Seek what? His kingdom and his righteousness. How then does being generous with our time translate into seeking his kingdom? Again, Jesus himself gives us the answer: "'Love the Lord your God with all your heart and with all your soul and with all your mind.' This is the first and greatest commandment. And the second is like it: 'Love your neighbor as yourself'" (Matthew 22:37–39).

## The Missed Opportunity

Our number-one priority is seeking God and following Him. Our pastor made that point in a sermon recently. His wife is a landscaper and owns a garden service. She takes care of our gardens, choosing and caring for the shrubs and roses, planting bulbs, perennials, and annuals. We recently added a deck to our home, and she designed a fern and woodland garden on the slope beside it. She ordered all the plants, but for some reason they were delivered to her house instead of ours.

She enlisted her husband, our pastor, to deliver them to our house because she needed to get them into the ground. Unfortunately, he already had a very busy day planned. As he dutifully unloaded the plants, Wayne came out to meet him and asked him to have a cup of coffee. The pastor, looking hurried and harried, said, "Perhaps another time." And with that he rushed off.

And then on Sunday he used my sweet husband as part of the sermon. Naturally he didn't use Wayne's name, but he said, "I had an opportunity I missed this week. God gave me an intersection, the same way He does for so many of us. I was so busy serving the church, I forgot to *be* the church."

What an important message for each one of us. We get so tied up with activities, committees, meetings, initiatives, and programs that are all well and good that we miss what's most important— people. We don't have time to notice that our neighbor is hurting. Or that there are people working in our office who are desperate to know the love of Christ. And the Lord says, "Seek first my kingdom . . ."

Earlier, I mentioned that the good is often the enemy of the best. My daughter Jennifer nailed it when she told me, "Remember, Mom, when you say yes to a speaking engagement or autographing, you're saying no to something else." Wise words. There are only so many hours in a day. So we must make a habit of carefully examining our choices. Just imagine how your decision making can be influenced if, when making choices between two seemingly "good" things, you ask yourself which would best result in seeking God and loving your neighbor.

## The Three-Thousand-Mile Conversation

If God and His kingdom come first, and neighbor comes second, I guess that our closest neighbors are the ones we live with—our families. I hate to think how often I inadvertently shortchange our family, because they are the ones who love and support me. I suppose that is partly because I know they are the ones most willing to cut me some slack.

Long ago I made a commitment to my marriage. Wayne and I recently celebrated forty years together. It would be misleading to say we've had the perfect marriage, because the truth is we haven't. Like all couples we've struggled. Over the years we've found small ways in which to keep our marriage fresh and healthy. Each night after dinner, we share a cup of coffee and talk about our day. Just ten minutes, sometimes longer. Those few minutes make all the difference.

Twice a year Wayne and I drive between our home in Washington State and our home in Florida. It takes about a week to travel three thousand three hundred and twenty-three miles. We treasure that time together. Six to seven days on the road, just the two of us, is a tune-up for our marriage. We often go long distances without saying a word, and then we'll chatter and laugh for two hundred miles straight. We both look forward to that time every December and June. It's the best vacation our marriage ever had.

Marriages go through seasons. Keeping a relationship strong takes an intentional commitment and time spent together—lots of time. Wayne and I have had our ups and downs, and we certainly hit some bad patches in our relationship. We are completely different people, and yet God brought us together. I'm certain that God's hand was instrumental in marrying Wayne and me because we were not Christians when we met. Still, there were signs of God's fingerprints all over our relationship. For one thing, Wayne did not come from a traditional family, and yet, totally out of character, he went to my father and formally asked permission to marry me. For me that became an important marker, because when I doubted (and, yes, there were times in those earlier years that I doubted that Wayne and I were together under God), I remembered that Wayne had gone to my father and my father had given Wayne his permission and his blessing to marry me.

We always believed marriage was for keeps, and though there were times we didn't think we'd make it, we stuck it out and grew together.

So, in the years since those first days, we have had to find ways to spend time together because our interests have always been different. For instance, Wayne loves poker. Yes, poker. (My apologies if that fact is offensive to some!) I can't think of anything that interests me less. I love anything to do with knitting—the patterns, the yarn, and the entire process of creating something for someone I love. There's nothing that interests Wayne less. So we have to find things we like to do together. I like to cook and Wayne loves to eat, but then again, so do I. We enjoy the same music, and often late at night we'll play music from the sixties and the seventies and sing at the top of our lungs, or dance across the floor until we are breathless with laughter. Wayne enjoys watching football, and that's perfect knitting time. Yes, we're different, but at the same time we've grown together, and all that growing, that process of becoming one, takes time.

Each night when I get home, the mundane stuff consumes a good chunk of time—things like preparing dinner and dealing with household matters that cropped up during the day, Wayne and I discovered it's not the time to talk and try to catch up. Instead, he comes in every night when I bathe and sits on the edge of the tub and we talk. And I love that. One of the things Wayne loves to do is rub lotion on my back when I come home from swimming.

My husband has a wonderful dry wit that never fails to make me laugh. Just recently he was rubbing my back with lotion and said, "Honey, you're getting an hourglass figure." He stopped for a moment before amending it. "Okay, an hour and fifteen minutes."

Another time our son, who was serving as an Airborne Ranger, told us about a mission he had been chosen for long after the fact. We were shocked that he had been selected for such a dangerous assignment. Wayne asked Ted why he hadn't said anything so that we could have been praying.

Ted said, "Dad, it's one of those situations where if I told you I'd have to kill you."

Without even a pause Wayne looked to me with a twinkle in his eyes and said, "Tell your mother."

Yes, it takes generous doses of time to cement a marriage.

Time and laughter.

## The Ten-Dollar Bill

The other day I heard author and humorist Ken Davis tell a story on his radio program *Lighten UP!* that illustrated how important it is for us to set aside time for our children. He told of a dad who was worn out from trying to keep a roof over his family and food on the table. He could hardly drag himself in the door at the end of the day, let alone interact with his small son. One evening his son stood by the door waiting and watching as the father came home from work.

"Daddy, how much money do you get paid for an hour of work?"

That was a sore spot. His father walked over to the recliner. "Twenty dollars an hour," he said. "And it's not enough, in case you're wondering. That's why I have to work so much overtime. Are you making a point here, son?"

"No, Daddy." The boy wrote the number down on a piece of paper and stood next to his father.

"Is there something else you want?" The dad felt tired and just wanted to turn on the television and forget the day.

The boy looked at his paper. "Can you loan me ten dollars?"

His father had had enough. "Go to your room and shut the door. I've had more than enough of your foolishness. I just told you how tight money is." He clenched his jaw as the little boy went silently to his room. "As if I've got money to throw around," he said to himself.

He sat there for a long time without turning the television on. He began to feel bad for lighting into his son. When he couldn't stand it any longer, he went to the child's room. His son lay face-down on the bed. "I'm sorry for getting mad, son. I'm tired. But if you need ten dollars for a toy or something, here it is." He held out a ten-dollar bill.

The little boy sat up and wiped his face. "It's not for a toy, Daddy." He reached under his pillow and pulled out a wad of crumpled bills and smoothed them out and added them to the ten-dollar bill. "I've been saving my dollars and now I have twenty of them." He smiled at his father as he held out the stack of money. "Can I buy an hour of time with you?"

Quality time with our children is paramount. How else will we pass along our values and connect with them on a deep level? It would be impossible without committing time with them one-on-one.

## *Discovery*

*Nothing says "You matter to me" more than the act of investing time with the people we care about.*

## The Birthday Bond

I now have eight grandchildren. I've already mentioned some of the things we do to keep them connected, but every year I take delight in knitting something special for each child. I like to take each one to a yarn store and let him or her pick out the yarn, the buttons, and the pattern. That way I know he or she is going to like it and wear it.

Cameron, my oldest grandson, isn't a real sweater person, but he loves army men. What fun we had finding a yarn that looked like camouflage when knitted. We went to the fabric store and bought military-looking badges, stars, and decorations that could be sewn onto the sweater after it was completed. It was sheer joy to create a one-of-a-kind knitting project for Cameron, but it was even more fun spending time with my one-of-a-kind grandson.

Madeline is one of my granddaughters. She's always been special to me because she was born on my birthday. Autumn is a busy travel time for me, and I missed her birthday two years in a row. One day she crawled up on my lap and said, "I don't want to have my birthday on your birthday anymore." I think she figured I was away because it was my birthday. She wanted me at her celebration.

When I saw how important it was to her, I said, "From now on, Maddy, I won't do anything on October twenty-second. That is our day." Since that time I've set aside our shared birthday and committed the time to spend with my granddaughter. And, boy, do we know how to have fun. I cannot help but wonder what ripple effect that decision will have in Maddy's life. Will she, too, invest herself in her children and grandchildren? Will she share with them the stories of shared birthdays? Oh I hope so!

## The Canasta Conundrum

So if we are setting priorities, after God and family next on the list would be the rest of God's people. I find myself very drawn to seniors. What a wealth of experience, maturity, and wisdom. As much as possible on Friday afternoons during the summer I drop by the Givens Senior Center and sit and knit with these wise and wonderful older ladies. Although time is always in short supply, I've learned that my life is richer if I spend part of my afternoon with my elders. I love those afternoons. And the women seem to enjoy my visits as well.

On one such afternoon the director asked to speak to me. She led me into her office and closed the door. *My goodness,* I thought, *is she going to ask me to leave because I was still in my fifties and not yet considered a senior?* She leaned forward and said in a low voice, "We've got a problem, Debbie."

I mentioned my Christmas teas in an earlier chapter. One of those teas has always been for my Givens Senior Center knitting ladies. How they love to come, wearing hats and gloves and their prettiest dresses. There's so much laughter around the table that it rings throughout the house. The tea is one I treasure.

So when the senior center director told me there was a problem, I wondered if my knitting ladies tea and afternoons at the center were over. But that wasn't it at all. Apparently the ladies who play canasta had sought her out. They said that the knitting ladies were "lording it over them" about my visits and the tea. I couldn't help but laugh.

"But I don't play canasta," I told the director. "I don't even know how to play canasta." Of course it wasn't about knitting or canasta, it was about time. So few people take time to spend with the seniors, the other ladies were hungry for it.

We solved the problem by inviting the canasta ladies to the tea as well. Knitting was no longer a prerequisite. So now all the ladies come, and I love having them to my house. The knitters bring their projects, and we do a show and tell. I come away thinking, *I want to knit that, and that, and that, and that.* It is time well spent. Over the years I've added other knitting friends I've made through the years. There are several authors who are knitters, so they come as well, in addition to five or six yarn store owners. We usually end up with about thirty-five or more at the Knitters' Tea—including, of course, a few canasta ladies.

## *Warm Up America!*

What if you could spend time relaxing doing something you absolutely love to do, with people who share your passion, and in the doing could dramatically improve the daily life of one person who desperately needs a little warmth and kindness in her life? I have found just the thing. Talk about God multiplying the bounty of time! One of my favorite foundations is Warm Up America! Knitters donate their time to create seven-by-nine-inch rectangles. Volunteers are encouraged to work with friends, coworkers, and family members to complete an afghan and donate it in their community. When that's not possible, the foundation's office serves as a collection point both for individual sections and for completed afghans.

The beauty of so many different participants is that a WUA! afghan resembles a patchwork quilt of many colors and textures, just as the participants and recipients represent the varied faces of America. The finished, brightly colored afghans are delivered to homeless, battered women's shelters and people in need.

Carl Sandburg once said, "Time is the coin of your life. It is the only coin you have, and only you can determine how it will be spent. Be careful lest you let other people spend it for you."

What he didn't say is that time is a gift from God. It is His gift to us. And our decision of how to invest the gift of time is our gift back to Him. Invest yourself in God's kingdom; love others by offering what feels like your too-limited measure of time and see what God does with it.

## Discovery

*God is the master of time. When we seek His wisdom on where to invest our time we are certain to invest well.*

# Simple Ways to Discover More Hours in Your Day

## Eliminate Time Wasters

❖ Television. Did you know that, on average, the American adult spends 2.5 hours a day watching television?[1] Just think, cutting television viewing in half would add 5 percent more time to your day. Eliminating television altogether would potentially give you more than 10 percent more time.

❖ Internet and e-mail. If we want to invest in the people we care about, we need to analyze where we spend our time. If Internet and e-mail are consuming more time than the people in our family, it's time to take stock.

❖ Chores. The mundane tasks we do each day eat up huge chunks of time. By investing some time and research into improving productivity and cutting needless steps, we can recoup some of that time.

## Multitask

❖ When I do sit down to watch television, I always take out my knitting. Doing two things at once makes me more productive.

❖ When Wayne and I take long road trips, we often listen to books on tape. It helps pass the time plus it gives us fodder for conversation.

❖ I often combine things on my to-do list with friend time. Christmas shopping with friends or going to a bookstore together just makes visiting all the more fun.

### Reclaim Lost Snippets of Time

❖ You'd be surprised at how much time you spend waiting. Always tuck a book in your purse or your pocket for those late appointments or time spent at school in the carpool queue.

❖ One friend does ankle-flexing exercises while waiting at long stoplights.

❖ Waiting for a pot to come to a boil? Write a note of encouragement to a friend.

### Put First Things First

But don't forget, the main reason for trying to find extra hours in our day is so that we can give them away to those things and those people who are important to us. In trying to be generous with our time, however, we need to be careful not to just keep piling new things on top of old things. G. K. Chesterton said it best: "The modern world has far too little understanding of the art of keeping young. Its notion of progress has been to pile one thing on top of another, without caring if each thing was crushed in turn. People forgot that the human soul can enjoy a thing most when there is time to think about it and be thankful for it. And by crowding things together they lost the sense of surprise; and surprise is the secret of joy."

**Do not be anxious about anything,**

**but in everything,**

**by prayer and petition, with thanksgiving,**

**present your requests to God.**

*Philippians 4:6*

Fourteen

# Red Stars, Research, and a Rolex

## The Offering of Prayer

An entire library could be written about prayer. Scratch that. An entire library *has* been written about prayer. But I want to explore only two facets of prayer. The first is praying that God would work generosity and kindness into our lives. The second is generously offering prayer on behalf of others, called intercession. Both kinds of prayer lead us more deeply into living in the spirit of generosity.

## Praying for a Generous Heart

Francis of Assisi prayed the following prayer: "O Divine Master, grant that I may not so much seek to be consoled as to console; to be understood as to understand; to be loved as to love; for it is in giving that we receive; it is in pardoning that we are pardoned; it is in dying that we are born to eternal life."

The most powerful prayers are when we ask God to change us instead of asking Him to change our circumstances. Isn't it strange that, while praying, we so seldom ask for change of character? We're usually asking for Him to work in our situation. It seems to me that we get this all backward.

I love St. Francis's prayer because it shifts the focus away from what we want and toward what we can do for others.

Pray that God will help us be generous. Ask Him to show us where He wants us to give. That He'll provide the resources with which to give. Such a prayer takes us out of ourselves and focuses us on God's heart instead of the desires of our hearts. We have already discovered that giving aligns us with the heart of God and is an act of worship. Here's where we ask Him to align us with His heart and teach us how to worship Him through giving. It's the kind of prayer He loves to answer.

## On Our Knees—and in Our Prayer Journal

In his book *Prayer*, Richard Foster says, "Intercession is a way of loving others. When we move from petition to intercession we are shifting our center of gravity from our own needs to the needs and concerns of others. Intercessory prayer is selfless prayer, even self-giving prayer."[1]

One of the ways God encourages me is through my prayer journal. Because I'm a writer it's so much easier for me to write my prayers, simply because I express myself best with the written word.

I've found that if I close my eyes and start to pray, my mind too often wanders. I'll be praying during my quiet time and my mind will move from, *Oh, thank you, Jesus, for everything you've done* to *What I should have for dinner tonight? What's in the freezer that I can use?* I have had to learn to be intentional with my prayers, and a prayer journal is what has worked for me.

Recently I was feeling discouraged because I had been praying for someone for a long time and had seen nothing change. It felt like my prayers smacked against the ceiling and lodged there. For whatever reason I started thumbing through the beginning of this year's prayer journal. I started with January first and read the prayers I had written. At the beginning of every month I write down specific prayers. Then I pray those prayers and add to them during the month.

I took a red pen and started marking off with big red stars all the prayers that had been answered. I made notations about how God had answered me. I wasn't into the exercise long before I recognized God's hand in each circumstance. I came away with a sense of awe, humbled by all He had done for me and my lack of recognition.

God used my prayer journal to encourage me at a low point. If you keep a list of prayer requests, you'll find the answers tucked in those entries. And you'll come away knowing how much God loves you and how He loves to listen to our prayers.

My friend also keeps a prayer journal. In the front is a section called "Remembering." Each time she starts a fresh journal, she moves this section over. In it, she keeps track of the long-term prayers of intercession. Every incident, every milestone gets recorded on those first few pages. She reports that it has helped her see God at work in her life. Sometimes she had prayed for one outcome that never happened, but as she began to track the progress of her prayers, a light bulb went on. "I kept praying for what seemed like the obvious path, and the whole time God was doing something far better," she said.

She's been tracking and remembering for more than ten years now, and she reports that her faith has grown by leaps and bounds. "Now when I watch something veer off the course I thought it should go, I start trying to figure out just what God has in mind."

## Letting Others Know You're Praying

When you get one of those assignments to pray for someone—one of those God nudges or divine appointments—don't be shy about letting the person know you are praying for him specifically. Few will take offense, no matter what their beliefs. Tell him even if you don't know why you are praying on his behalf. Some of the most exciting connections come about when you just say, "I don't know why, but I've felt a need to pray for you this week."

People are touched. More often than not, something is happening in their lives—maybe something they've told no one—and finding out that God set you to praying is just what they need to realize that He is still in control. That He cares about them and their problems.

I was doing a book autographing in the Philadelphia area and two members of the publicity team were with me. Think top Madison Avenue publicists, New York born and bred. They help keep everything professional, polished, and moving.

A woman came up to the table with her book for me to sign. She'd obviously gone through treatment for cancer. She wore a chemo cap and she told me how much reading my books had helped her get through her chemotherapy. She said she could forget about how sick she was feeling when she escaped into my books. She had stood in line for a long time to let me know that. It couldn't have been easy, but she wanted to encourage me.

She did. More than she could ever know.

I came around the table, took both of her hands, and prayed with her. I didn't even think about what it would look like to my publicity team, the bookseller, or the people in line. When I finished and we had hugged, I remembered everyone else and our surroundings. Not a single person in line seemed impatient. I could see my two publicists crying openly. The impromptu prayer in the aisle of a bookstore hadn't put anyone off in any way. As I sat down, I silently thanked God for giving me the ability to write—to be able to touch people where they are hurting. It humbled me.

## Watching God at Work

My friend Sheila Rabe is a wonderful writer, but she went through a dry spell. She couldn't seem to sell anything. She had promised her son if he went to a Christian college, she would pay his tuition. And here he was about to enroll, and she hadn't sold a word for nearly a year. Sheila and I spent hours brainstorming book ideas, bouncing them off of each other. I was doing the best I could to help her, but everything came to a dead end. It didn't make any sense.

One day she called. I could hear the excitement in her voice. "We've got to have lunch," she said. I just knew she had sold something.

So when we sat down I said, "Tell me, tell me. What did you sell?"

Smiling boldly she met my look, "Nothing. I've sold absolutely nothing."

I think my mouth must have sagged open.

"I was praying," Shelia went on to explain, "and it came to me that every time God did a major work in one of the lives of His people in the Bible, He changed his name. Abram became Abraham. Saul became Paul. Peter became the Rock. Or Simon became Peter." And then she added, "I've decided I'm changing my name. From this moment forward I'm Sheila the Faithful. I'm going to remain faithful to God, and I know that He will remain faithful to me."

And guess what? She didn't sell the entire time that her son was in college. Four long years. But God was faithful, and she never once missed a single tuition payment. She got odd jobs. She taught classes. Somehow the payment was always there when needed. After her son graduated she sold, and she sold big.

Sheila opened her hands, trusting that God would give her the resources. She believed long before she had any idea how God would work.

## *Prayer Works*

Researchers at Duke University Medical Center used rigorous scientific methods to study the therapeutic value of prayer. The results appeared in the *American Heart Journal,* November 1, 2001. One hundred and fifty patients with acute coronary insufficiency were enrolled in the study. All were scheduled for angioplasty—where doctors use a balloon device to force open a narrowed artery— followed by coronary artery stenting. That's where a mesh tube is inserted into the artery to keep it open. All the patients were cared for in the coronary intensive care unit. Patients, doctors, and nurses did not know which group patients were in. Prayer group members were scattered around the nation and given only the first names, diagnoses, and prognoses of patients. The prayed-for group had 25 to 30 percent fewer complications than the not-prayed-for group. And those who receive intercessory prayer (instead of other meditative therapies like healing touch or guided imagery) had the greatest therapeutic benefits.

Remember the story about Wayne's friend Norm? When he was in the hospital, none of us expected him to live. He had become septic, which means he had poisoning in the blood. It is a killer. Plus he suffered two heart attacks while he was hospitalized. His kidneys quit functioning; he had pneumonia in both lungs. They couldn't even get a read on his blood pressure.

We interceded for him day and night. People in our church prayed.

Before Norm had gone to the hospital, he had somehow lost his watch. The family had torn their house apart looking for his watch. It was expensive, his prized possession, and it just felt like another piece of him that was lost.

His daughters sat in the hospital for hours. Over and over they would say, "Dad, we love you. Don't give up. Mom needs you. We don't want you to die. You've got to fight, Dad. You've got to fight." As they talked to him and prayed, his blood pressure went up and eventually evened out.

The next day as his youngest daughter, Chrissy, drove to the family home for a badly needed break, she just broke down, sobbing. She just didn't see how she could lose her dad. She parked the car outside the house and sat in her vehicle and prayed. "I hate to be so weak, God, but I need a sign, let me know everything's going to be all right, that no matter what happens, I can accept Your will and that I can take care of my mom."

When Chrissy finished praying and got out of the car, something caught her eye over by the garbage can—something that sparkled in the sun. She went to investigate. There on the ground was her father's Rolex. They had searched every inch of the property, but there it was. She had asked for reassurance—for a sign—as she prayed for her father. For her, finding that lost wristwatch gave her the hope she needed to get through the long ordeal until her dad could finally come home.

Lord Jesus, You honor a generous heart and one that gives freely. May we learn to give more and demand less. Enable us to do more letting go and less holding on. May we simply yield to Your sweet spirit of generosity and in so doing relinquish that part of us that fears not being in control. Take the reins from our grasp and teach us to rest in that release. Amen.

## *Discovery*

*The act of prayer aligns us with the very heart of God.*
*The simple truth is that it is God*
*Who is generous to us in hearing our every prayer.*

## SIMPLE ACTS OF PRAYER

Sometimes the hardest part of embarking on a prayer journey is making it an everyday part of life. Nothing will enrich us or help us align ourselves with the heart of God more than regular prayer. Here are a few things that have helped me:

✦ *Regular place.* It helps me to have a regular place where I read my Bible and pray. I use my kitchen table even though I have so many different wonderful nooks in my house. It's just that I've used that spot for so long, it feels like the place I meet God every morning. Some of my friends love to light candles and create a set-apart feeling. Whatever works.

❖ *Regular time.* For me this is important. I have a routine. I get up while it's still dark and meet God as the sun rises. You might be a vespers kind of person or a night owl.

❖ *Combining prayer with Bible reading.* I love combining the two because God so often speaks to me through my Bible reading or my devotional.

❖ *Using a prayer journal.* I've already shared about using a journal. One young Salvation Army girl around the turn of the century in England used to write her prayers on scraps of paper and tack them to her wall. When the prayer was answered, she'd take it down and put it in a box. The longer she served God, the fuller her box became. What a legacy!

❖ *Tandem prayer.* If solitary prayer is too lonely for you, find a prayer partner. You can pray over the phone, online, or in person.

Here's the goal: "Pray without ceasing" (1 Thessalonians 5:17; King James Version).

*Always be prepared to give an answer*

*to everyone who asks you to give the*

*reason for the hope that you have.*

*But do this with gentleness and respect.*

1 Peter 3:15

## Fifteen

# A Question, an Opportunity, and a Conversation Worth Having

### The Sharing of Our Faith Stories

I was flying to California a couple of weeks ago. I had brought along a newsletter from the Guideposts Positive Thinkers Club. In it Ruth Stafford Peale told the story of a woman going into a hair salon in Nashville. She sat down in the reception area to wait. There, with all the magazines, sat a Bible. Now she'd seen many Bibles before, but there were tabs in this Bible like you would put on a file folder, numbered one through eight. She picked up the Bible and turned to the tab marked one and read the underscored passage. Then she went to two. And three. All the way through number eight.

It didn't take her long to realize that each passage was a tracing of the origin of sin and God's answer to conquer that sin and bring people back into friendship with Him. As she came to the end of the readings, she turned to the back of the Bible. It said, "You have now read the Plan of Salvation. God loves you. He's waiting for you. He wants to claim you as His child. Are you ready to accept Him? If so, put your name here." And guess what followed that? A list of names! Clients waiting to have their hair cut had read those verses, realized they wanted friendship with God for all eternity, and made a decision right there to begin a relationship with Jesus.

She asked the receptionist about the Bible. The woman said, "Oh one of our clients, a young businesswoman, did that. She asked if she could leave this Bible in our reception area."

Isn't that a wonderful gift? The young woman who brought the tabbed Bible to the patrons of a beauty shop treasured her friendship with God so much that she wanted to share it with others. She was showing someone the path to find Jesus Christ in a beauty salon and she did so by simply leaving the Bible there for whoever was interested to pick up and read.

Have you ever noticed how easy it can be to chatter and make small talk, but how reluctant we can be to have spiritual conversations with others? We all have a spiritual story to tell—questions and experiences that run deep about our purpose, the meaning of our existence, and our understanding about the God who created us. Why do you suppose that we hold back when it comes to speaking of such things?

The term "performance anxiety" is not usually applied to sharing our faith stories, but too often we get tangled up in things like approach, relevancy, ease of presentation, and similar complications. It seems that the more sophisticated we become, the more befuddled we get about what some call witnessing—giving witness to what we have experienced in our relationship with God.

It can be as simple as telling someone about a great book we read or a favorite television show. If we seek to live in a spirit of generosity, we'll open our hearts and tell people about the very best things in our lives. Or, if uncertain about what to believe, we will open our hearts and share our biggest questions. Can you imagine a more important conversation to have?

Speaking for myself, I find that when I speak about what Jesus has personally done for me, then it is actually quite easy to share with others. After all, I am simply talking to others about the most important relationship in my life—my relationship with the God who made me and loves me.

## The Ultimate Rescue

We've heard so many stories from the ill-fated *Titanic*, but I treasure the one about the young preacher John Harper. The widower Reverend Harper had sailed from London to preach for several months at the Moody Church in Chicago. He traveled with his six-year-old daughter, Nana, and her nurse, Miss Leitch.

It was a frigid night on April 14, 1912, when the ship struck the iceberg and the sea poured in. John Harper gathered his small daughter and managed to get her into the eleventh lifeboat. The nurse followed. He kissed his daughter, Nana, and told her that he'd see her again someday.

According to later reports many saw him wearing a life jacket, making his way up and down the decks, helping people into lifeboats. He yelled, "Women, children, and the unsaved into lifeboats." Soon afterward the ship began to creak and split, throwing people into the bitterly cold waters.

Reverend Harper was seen frantically swimming from person to person, leading them to Jesus before hypothermia claimed them and they slipped beneath the water. He came up to one young man who was very near shock. Reverend Harper tried to address matters of his soul but the man resisted, so John Harper swam away to minister to others. When he finally came back to the young man, Reverend Harper took off his life jacket. He fastened it around the man, saying, "You need this more than I do." One more time he witnessed to the young man, who finally accepted the gift of salvation that his persistent rescuer offered.

Of the 1,528 persons who ended up in the water that night, only six were rescued by the lifeboats. The young man was one of them. At a survivors meeting four years later, he stood up and told the story. He recounted the last words John Harper said before going under: "Believe on the name of the Lord Jesus and you will be saved."[1]

You may not share your faith in such an in-your-face sort of manner, but desperate times don't leave much room for nuanced discussions about faith. The truth is, we live in desperate times. I'm not saying people are in the water ready to slip under in minutes, but as we discussed earlier, we are all eternal beings on a short assignment while here on earth. Eventually we will all die. And each one of us needs rescue.

If that's true, what are some other ways to share our faith stories generously with people? What are some ways to engage in meaningful conversations about our spiritual lives? I think we can take some cues from the story of Philip and the Ethiopian found in the Bible. Taking the passage apart helps us see that talking about our spiritual lives need not be complicated.

## *Wait for the Prompting of the Holy Spirit*

Before we even think about diving in, we need to listen for the prompting of the Holy Spirit. In Acts 8:26–29, Philip has no trouble hearing the voice of God: "Now an angel of the Lord said to Philip, 'Go south to the road—the desert road—that goes down from Jerusalem to Gaza.'" So he started out, and on his way he met an Ethiopian eunuch, an important official in charge of all the treasury of Candace, queen of the Ethiopians. This man had gone to Jerusalem to worship, and on his way home was sitting in his chariot reading the book of Isaiah the prophet. The Spirit told Philip, 'Go to that chariot and stay near it.'"

We may not hear the prompting quite so audibly, but if we are tuned in, we'll recognize it. Sometimes it comes with a heightened awareness—"Look at that woman, sitting all alone on that bench. She looks troubled." Or, as we pray, our mind continues to stray toward one friend.

The reason it's important to listen for God's prompting is because we need the Holy Spirit's groundwork before we dive into sharing our faith. To paraphrase Henry T. Blackaby in *Experiencing God*: God is already at work around us; we need to pay attention and move alongside Him.

## *Observe and Ask Questions*

Even though Philip knew he had a divine mandate, he proceeded gently. "Then Philip ran up to the chariot and heard the man reading Isaiah the prophet. 'Do you understand what you are reading?' Philip asked. 'How can I,' he said, 'unless someone explains it to me?' So he invited Philip to come up and sit with him" (Acts 8:30–31).

I love this! The Ethiopian wasn't sure what he believed, but he was spiritually interested and curious. And he responded to an invitation to discuss spiritual truth. All he needed was someone to offer! It may be easier simply to deliver some practiced speech, but it is so much more effective to ask a question. Philip showed interest, he asked a question, and then he waited for the answer. He tested the Ethiopian's openness and his responsiveness to hearing the gospel by posing it in the form of a question.

## Listen, Listen, Listen

Yes, listening again. And isn't listening the hardest part? The nicest thing about using Philip's model of sharing your faith story is that we listen to the other person instead of launching into a complicated argument for faith. I'm a little theologically challenged, so I'm happy to read the words of the great apologist C. S. Lewis in one of his letters: "Apologetic work is so dangerous to one's own faith. A doctrine never seems dimmer to me than when I have just successfully defended it."

I can listen to my friend's questions even if I cannot explain the whys and the hows of God. I don't need to know the answers. My part is simply to introduce my friend to the One Who has all the answers.

### Meet Their Needs

The Ethiopian was searching. He needed an explanation. Philip could answer his questions. Meeting needs is what generosity is all about. We will never know how many people accepted the good news of salvation because first their human needs were addressed. I've heard missionaries speak about their work, and one of the first things they explain is how essential it is to meet the dire needs of those they've come to serve before they can share the truth of God's love.

## Enter Their World

"So he invited Philip to come up and sit with him" (verse 31). This is where we sometimes stumble. In our divided world, we often try to keep the "sacred" and the "secular" apart—church folk on one side, worldly folk on the other. That's a mistake. I'm beginning to learn that if I'm not willing to come alongside someone—to put my arm around her and enter her world—I'm probably not where the Lord wants me to be in relation to her. The truth is, I'm probably not where He wants me to be in relation to Him, either.

## Engage Them at Their Point of Interest

Take a look at Acts 8:34–35. "The eunuch asked Philip, 'Tell me, please, who is the prophet talking about, himself or someone else?' Then Philip began with that very passage of Scripture and told him the good news about Jesus." What a lesson for us. The Ethiopian asked a specific question, and Philip began at that point and gave him the gospel. Philip's message came easily and naturally in answer to a specific question and a deeply felt need. That's when we know the Lord got there first and we just came alongside to join Him.

## Travel with Them on the Journey

Hit-and-run evangelism wasn't Philip's style. The passage goes on to tell us: "As they traveled along the road, they came to some water and the eunuch said, 'Look, here is water. Why shouldn't I be baptized?' And he gave orders to stop the chariot. Then both

Philip and the eunuch went down into the water and Philip baptized him" (Acts 8:36–38). Philip didn't just have a conversation
with the Ethiopian, he traveled for a time with him.

Sharing our faith story often takes time and relationship building. If we are committed to living generously, then we need to be
equally generous with the Good News. There's no need to get
caught up in theology or apologetics. It just takes time and a willingness to ask questions, to meet needs, and to travel along the
journey for a time. And it is something we can all do if we just
listen for the prompting of the Holy Spirit.

## *Discovery*

*Sharing our faith stories is truly far simpler than we imagine it to be.
After all, God is already at work in the lives of those around us.
We need only to share what God is doing in our own lives to
open the door for meaningful conversation.*

## THE SIMPLE TRUTH OF FAITH

That tabbed Bible at the beauty salon, giving the verses that lead the way to faith may have used the following verses:

### The Only Way to Heaven

"Jesus answered, 'I am the way and the truth and the life. No one comes to the Father except through me.'" (John 14:6)

### Good Works Cannot Save You

"For it is by grace you have been saved, through faith—and this not from yourselves, it is the gift of God—not by works, so that no one can boast." (Ephesians 2:8–9)

### Trust Jesus Christ Today

Here's how to begin a friendship with God:

*Admit you are a sinner.*

✦ "For all have sinned and fall short of the glory of God." (Romans 3:23)

✦ "Therefore, just as sin entered the world through one man, and death through sin, and in this way death came to all men, because all sinned." (Romans 5:12)

✦ "If we claim we have not sinned, we make him out to be a liar and his word has no place in our lives." (1 John 1:10)

*(Continued)*

*Be willing to turn from sin (repent).*

✦ "I tell you, no! But unless you repent, you too will all perish." (Luke 13:5)

✦ "In the past God overlooked such ignorance, but now he commands all people everywhere to repent." (Acts 17:30)

*Believe that Jesus Christ died for you, was buried, and rose from the dead.*

✦ "For God so loved the world that he gave his one and only Son, that whoever believes in him shall not perish but have eternal life." (John 3:16)

✦ "But God demonstrates his own love for us in this: While we were still sinners, Christ died for us." (Romans 5:8)

✦ "That if thou shalt confess with thy mouth the Lord Jesus, and shalt believe in thine heart that God hath raised him from the dead, thou shalt be saved." (Romans 10:9; King James Version)

*Through prayer, invite Jesus into your life to become your personal Savior.*

✦ "For it is with your heart that you believe and are justified, and it is with your mouth that you confess and are saved." (Romans 10:10)

✧ "Everyone who calls on the name of the Lord will be saved." (Romans 10:13)

*What to pray:*
"Dear God, I am a sinner and need forgiveness. I believe that Jesus Christ shed His precious blood and died for my sin. I am willing to turn from sin. I now invite Jesus to come into my heart and life as my personal Savior."

✧ "Yet to all who received Him, to those who believed in his name, he gave the right to become children of God." (John 1:12)

✧ "Therefore, if anyone is in Christ, he is a new creation; the old has gone, the new has come!" (2 Corinthians 5:17)

**Whatever you do,**

**whether in word or deed, do it all in the**

**name of the Lord Jesus, giving thanks to God**

**the Father through him.**

*Colossians 3:17*

## Sixteen

# A Treasure, a Shawl, and a Hymn over the Phone

## The Heart of Service

So what happens if you give and give until you have nothing left? Do you become nothing more than a servant to others? Here's the irony: no one is richer than God's servants. The funny thing is that no matter how hard we try to give, God continually gives us more.

The Bible tells us that we cannot store up treasures here on earth—moths and rust make short work of them. But we forget the second half of that verse—we *can* store up treasures in heaven. You've always heard that we can't take it with us. I'm hoping by now we've exploded that myth—we *can* take it with us.

## Watch the Helpers

After the bombing of the twin towers of New York's World Trade Center, the nation was stunned. Parents didn't know what to say to their children. They'd seen such evil things on television that even adults couldn't put the events into any kind of context. When a few parents wrote to Mr. Rogers, the beloved children's television personality, to ask for advice, Fred Rogers said, "Tell them to watch the helpers." What wise advice. I've thought about his answer many times. When tragedy hits, don't focus on the faces of pain and horror. Let your eyes follow those who are rescuing, feeding, healing, sweeping, comforting, and rebuilding. On 9/11, it was the selfless firefighters who took center stage. They will be remembered long after the evildoers are forgotten.

## Rolling up Our Sleeves

As you can probably tell from the number of times I've mentioned her, I've long admired Ruth Stafford Peale. She was guided by this belief: "I consider it a priority anything that helps another person." That kind of other-centeredness is rare these days.

There are few gifts as precious as the gift of service. I treasure the letter I received from one of my readers, Amanda W. I met her at a book signing in Georgia. She told me about her service group that was started because of reading one of my books. I asked her to e-mail me with some of the things they've done. Here's what she wrote:

*We meet once a month. Our goal is to help as many people in our community as we can. While we are focusing on our com-*

munity that does not mean we won't help people in other areas of the county or world for that matter.

Here are some of the things we've done so far:

• *We've made freezer meals. We assemble a dozen to eighteen complete meals each time we gather. We keep our freezers stocked so we can give these meals to those in our area who have ongoing illness in their families. We've also given them to families who were in the process of moving and several families who just needed to know that someone cares. We have people who keep these meals in their freezer. They can be heated and delivered hot and ready in just a short time. This has been a lot of fun for those of us putting the meals together.*

• *We have made loomed, knitted, and crocheted hats to donate to the center where one of the ladies at our church is getting chemo. Our goal for the first month was fifty hats. I think we only ended up with thirty, but what has happened is that the ladies are still making hats and have been for the last several months. Our total is up to about sixty hats now. It's been fun to teach the ladies who want to learn how to knit or crochet and see them catch the bug! It is also so wonderful to see those who think they aren't "crafty" to realize that they can use a loom to make a hat and then see them share it with their families. We are having kids bring in hats or the moms come in and tell us that the hats were made by a son or daughter. This has been a great way to have the whole family give service to others.*

• *We made a scripture quilt for a lady who has struggled for the past several years with health issues. Last July she was in a coma for over a month, but she was at church for the first time this past Sunday and it was really a joyous occasion. We all chose our favorite scripture. One of our ladies has a computerized sewing machine that she can program. She embroidered each scripture on a quilt square and then we hand-tied the quilt.*

*• One month we gathered some young men and women together and helped clean up the yard of a family whose dad has been sick and couldn't work. The mom has been working long hours and trying to do everything. After we were done mowing, raking, planting flowers and other general yard work, one of the boys noticed that the house next door's yard needed to be mowed also. He asked if he could mow that one too! All the boys that had brought mowers went over and mowed that lawn and got it done in no time flat! I was so proud that they saw a need and followed through.*

*• This month we are collecting school supplies to donate to kids that are in foster care.*

*• Next month we are going to an assisted living home and playing games with the residents.*

*I am not sure what else will come along; it seems that just when we are trying to think what we can do next, something comes along that is just right for our little group.*

What a testimony to service. I find it amazing to consider how God is multiplying their work. Former congresswoman Pat Schroeder said, "You can't wring your hands and roll up your sleeves at the same time."

That's what touched me so deeply about Amanda W.'s church group. While everyone else stands around wringing their hands about the state of the world, these servants are rolling up their sleeves and quietly changing it. Bravo!

## The Work of Their Hands

Earlier this year, I received a beautiful hand-knit prayer shawl with this note: "Since 1998 Shawl Ministry has spread around the world, with groups gathering to pray and knit for those in need and those celebrating life's joys. As they create shawls for others, their handiwork becomes an expression of their love—and the loving care of God who works through them. Shawls console those who are grieving, comfort those who are ill, bring hope to those in despair."

My shawl was knit by Connie Heinfeld of the New Haven United Methodist Church, but thirteen members of their group had signed the letter that said, "The following individuals gathered around this shawl, laying praying hands upon it, blessing it and you with loving hearts and asking for God's continued presence in your life."

My book *Back on Blossom Street* centered on just such a group of women knitting prayer shawls. I treasure that shawl and the prayers that came with it. I also treasure the works of these ladies' hands—the gift of service.

Another reader, Marilyn Thomsen from Nebraska, wrote in an e-mail: "I just finished reading *Back on Blossom Street*. I've knitted/ crocheted about sixty-five prayer shawls over the last two years. Our church has given out over one hundred now. We pray over them (for the recipient) as we knit/crochet them. Then a group of women (Lord's Laughing Ladies who meet for breakfast every other Friday) prays over them (both for the recipients and the ones who made them). We've been keeping a scrapbook of pictures of all the recipients (not limited to members of our congregation). We keep hearing from the recipients about how they were touched and how they love their prayer shawls."

## Offer Your Loaves and Fishes

One of the themes of this book has been to offer what you have—to bring the loaves and fishes of your resources no matter how modest. An elderly widow did just that. Restricted in her activities, she was nonetheless eager to serve the Lord. After praying about this, she realized that she could bring blessing to others by playing the piano. The next day she placed this small ad in the *Oakland Tribune*: "Pianist will play hymns by phone daily for those who are sick and despondent—the service is free."

The notice included the number to dial. When people called, she would ask, "What hymn would you like to hear?" Within a few months her playing had brought cheer to several hundred people. Many of them freely poured out their hearts to her, and she was able to help and encourage them.

## A Weekday Faith

If the church is going to be relevant, we need to roll up our sleeves and offer service to a hurting world. That world no longer has patience with a Sunday Christian. They're looking to see Christians who live out their faith.

Writer, artist, and philosopher Elbert Hubbard wrote, "Remember the weekday to keep it holy."

As Jason Zahariades said on the blog The Off Ramp, "The church is God's sent people. That means when everything is stripped away—the building, the events, the activities, the leaders, and other identifying markers for the church—the people are the church and church is the people. Therefore, wherever God's people are corporately or individually, there is the church. Church is at home, in the car, in the restaurant, the beach—wherever God's people find themselves in their daily lives."[1]

Like my pastor keeps saying, "We don't want to go to church or do church, we want to *be* the church."

## Who Is My Neighbor?

In Luke 10:27–37, one of the learned men of the day decided to test Jesus. He first asked what he must do to inherit eternal life. Jesus responded by asking him, "What is written in God's law? How do you interpret it?" The man answered, "That you love the Lord your God with all your passion and prayer and muscle and intelligence—and that you love your neighbor as well as you do yourself."

"You have answered correctly," Jesus replied. "Do this and you will live."

But he wanted to justify himself, so he asked Jesus, "And who is my neighbor?"

In reply Jesus said: "A man was going down from Jerusalem to Jericho, when he fell into the hands of robbers. They stripped him of his clothes, beat him and went away, leaving him half dead. A priest happened to be going down the same road, and when he saw the man, he passed by on the other side. So too, a Levite, when he came to the place and saw him, passed by on the other side. But a Samaritan, as he traveled, came where the man was; and when he saw him, he took pity on him. He went to him and bandaged his wounds, pouring on oil and wine. Then he put the man on his own donkey, took him to an inn and took care of him. The next day he took out two silver coins and gave them to the innkeeper. 'Look after him,' he said, 'and when I return, I will reimburse you for any extra expense you may have.'

"Which of these three do you think was a neighbor to the man who fell into the hands of robbers?"

The expert in the law replied, "The one who had mercy on him." Jesus told him, "Go and do likewise."

Catherine Booth was the mother of the Salvation Army. "Wherever Catherine Booth went," said G. Campbell Morgan, the famous nineteenth-century minister, "humanity went to hear her. Princes and peeresses merged with paupers and prostitutes."

One night, Morgan shared in a meeting with Mrs. Booth, and a great crowd of "publicans and sinners" was there. Her message brought many into friendship with God. After the meeting, Morgan and Mrs. Booth went to be entertained at a fine home, and the lady of the manor said, "My dear Mrs. Booth, that meeting was dreadful."

"What do you mean, dearie?" asked Mrs. Booth.

"Oh, when you were speaking, I was looking at those people opposite to me. Their faces were so terrible, many of them. I don't think I shall sleep tonight!"

"Why, dearie, don't you know them?" Mrs. Booth asked, and the hostess replied, "Certainly not!"

"Well, that is interesting," Mrs. Booth said. "I did not bring them with me from London; they are your neighbors!"

If we are going to seek a servant's heart, we're going to need to reach out to our neighbors, in the largest sense of the word.

John Wesley's rule states our mission of service succinctly:

Do all the good you can,
By all the means you can,
In all the ways you can,

In all the places you can,
At all the times you can,
To all the people you can,
As long as ever you can.

## Ten Rules for Happier Living

I wish I knew who penned these rules for happier living. They've been repeated often, but they are wise words for us as we seek to live in the spirit of generosity.

**1.** Give something away—no strings attached.

**2.** Do a kindness—and forget it.

**3.** Spend a few minutes with the aged—their experience is priceless guidance.

**4.** Look intently into the face of a baby—and marvel.

**5.** Laugh often—it's life's lubricant.

**6.** Give thanks—a thousand times a day is not enough.

**7.** Pray—or you will lose the way.

**8.** Work—with vim and vigor.

**9.** Plan as though you'll live forever—because you will.

**10.** Live as though you'll die tomorrow—because you will, on some tomorrow.

## Discovery

*The best way for us to share the lifestyle of generosity is to model it.
The heart that chooses to serve others will multiply the happiness in this
world and reap the eternal reward of joy in heaven. Such a heart is
aligned with the very heart of God.*

## SIMPLE ACTS OF GENEROSITY

I hope you have found the stories and principles we have discussed in these chapters inspiring. I know that recounting and exploring them has spurred me on to live the generous life more deliberately. As you take one final look at the ways we can be generous, may you be reminded that one simple act of generosity can change a life, a community, and the world. And every act, no matter how small, gives back to the giver and moves us closer to the very heart of God. Please write to me and let me know of your experiences with generosity. I would love to celebrate the ripple effects as God multiplies your loaves and fishes!

❖ Leap from the springboard of gratitude.

❖ Participate in the mystery of sharing.

❖ Perform acts of encouragement.

❖ Develop the habit of good deeds.

❖ Expand the impact of forgiveness.

◈ Release the power of believing the best.

◈ Experience the bounty of open-handed giving.

◈ Practice the art of listening.

◈ Celebrate the privilege of inspiring hope.

◈ Share the spirit of Christmas.

◈ Bestow the gift of caregiving.

◈ Donate the bounty of time.

◈ Present the offering of prayer.

◈ Enjoy the sharing of faith stories.

◈ Cultivate the heart of service.

◈ Give God the last word in how you invest your life.

**Let the word of Christ dwell in you richly**

**as you teach and admonish one another**

**with all wisdom,**

**and as you sing psalms, hymns**

**and spiritual songs**

**with gratitude in your hearts to God.**

*Colossians 3:16*

# Seventeen

# *Giving God the Last Word*

Throughout this book we've explored what it means to live in the spirit of generosity. We've talked about being generous in acts of gratitude, sharing, encouragement, good deeds, forgiveness, seeing others through God's eyes, giving, listening, hospitality, hope, celebrating, caring for others, taking time for the eternal things, prayer, sharing our faith stories, and serving.

Yet we've only scratched the surface.

There are five things I know for sure. Those are:

~ Giving not only changes the recipient, it changes us.

~ Giving aligns us with the very heartbeat of God.

~ The Bible says that we *can* take it with us.

~ We are called to give—cheerfully and joyfully.

~ Giving is an act of worship.

I'm praying that, through the pages of this book, you discovered the power of generosity. I hope you have been inspired to dedicate yourself to acts of generosity. Seeing that you've stuck it out with me this far, I pray that you'll be willing to commit your resources to eternal goals.

But I don't want to have the last word. Let's see what Jesus says about living in the spirit of generosity. The whole chapter of Matthew 6 (as rendered in *The Message*) sums up the truths we have explored together.

## Giving to the Needy

*1* "Be especially careful when you are trying to be good so that you don't make a performance out of it. It might be good theater, but the God who made you won't be applauding. *2–4* "When you do something for someone else, don't call attention to yourself. You've seen them in action, I'm sure—'playactors' I call them—treating prayer meeting and street corner alike as a stage, acting compassionate as long as someone is watching, playing to the crowds. They get applause, true, but that's all they get. When you help someone out, don't think about how it looks. Just do it—quietly and unobtrusively. That is the way your God, who conceived you in love, working behind the scenes, helps you out.

## Prayer

*5* "And when you come before God, don't turn that into a theatrical production either. All these people making a regular show out of their prayers, hoping for stardom! Do you think God sits in a box seat?

6 "Here's what I want you to do: Find a quiet, secluded place so you won't be tempted to role-play before God. Just be there as simply and honestly as you can manage. The focus will shift from you to God, and you will begin to sense his grace.

7–13 "The world is full of so-called prayer warriors who are prayer-ignorant. They're full of formulas and programs and advice, peddling techniques for getting what you want from God. Don't fall for that nonsense. This is your Father you are dealing with, and he knows better than you what you need. With a God like this loving you, you can pray very simply. Like this:

> Our Father in heaven,
> Reveal who you are.
> Set the world right;
> Do what's best—as above, so below.
> Keep us alive with three square meals.
> Keep us forgiven with you and forgiving others.
> Keep us safe from ourselves and the Devil.
> You're in charge!
> You can do anything you want!
> You're ablaze in beauty!
> Yes. Yes. Yes.

14–15 "In prayer there is a connection between what God does and what you do. You can't get forgiveness from God, for instance, without also forgiving others. If you refuse to do your part, you cut yourself off from God's part.

## Fasting

*16–18* "When you practice some appetite-denying discipline to better concentrate on God, don't make a production out of it. It might turn you into a small-time celebrity but it won't make you a saint. If you 'go into training' inwardly, act normal outwardly. Shampoo and comb your hair, brush your teeth, wash your face. God doesn't require attention-getting devices. He won't overlook what you are doing; he'll reward you well.

## Treasures in Heaven

*19–21* "Don't hoard treasure down here where it gets eaten by moths and corroded by rust or—worse!—stolen by burglars. Stockpile treasure in heaven, where it's safe from moth and rust and burglars. It's obvious, isn't it? The place where your treasure is, is the place you will most want to be, and end up being.

*22–23* "Your eyes are windows into your body. If you open your eyes wide in wonder and belief, your body fills up with light. If you live squinty-eyed in greed and distrust, your body is a dank cellar. If you pull the blinds on your windows, what a dark life you will have!

*24* "You can't worship two gods at once. Loving one god, you'll end up hating the other. Adoration of one feeds contempt for the other. You can't worship God and Money both.

## Do Not Worry

*25–26* "If you decide for God, living a life of God-worship, it follows that you don't fuss about what's on the table at mealtimes or whether the clothes in your closet are in fashion. There is far more to your life than the food you put in your stomach, more to your outer appearance than the clothes you hang on your body. Look at the birds, free and unfettered, not tied down to a job description, careless in the care of God. And you count far more to him than birds.

27–29 "Has anyone by fussing in front of the mirror ever gotten taller by so much as an inch? All this time and money wasted on fashion—do you think it makes that much difference? Instead of looking at the fashions, walk out into the fields and look at the wildflowers. They never primp or shop, but have you ever seen color and design quite like it? The ten best-dressed men and women in the country look shabby alongside them.

30–33 "If God gives such attention to the appearance of wildflowers—most of which are never even seen—don't you think he'll attend to you, take pride in you, do his best for you? What I'm trying to do here is to get you to relax, to not be so preoccupied with *getting*, so you can respond to God's *giving*. People who don't know God and the way he works fuss over these things, but you know both God and how he works. Steep your life in God-reality, God-initiative, God-provisions. Don't worry about missing out. You'll find all your everyday human concerns will be met.

34 "Give your entire attention to what God is doing right now, and don't get worked up about what may or may not happen tomorrow. God will help you deal with whatever hard things come up when the time comes.

We each have a long way to go, but if we commit to just one simple act, miraculous things will happen. I can't wait to see what the Lord does with our offering. Heaven will be richer because we will have discovered that we can, indeed, take it with us. When we see the ripple effect and experience the real power of generosity, our lives will be changed forever.

# Acknowledgments

Most readers skip these pages, as they are often a list of names that mean nothing to those purchasing the book and everything to the author. My hope is that you will be interested enough to scan the next few lines.

People often say, "God bless you." I have a ready response when they do. I tell them, "He already has." I confess, I live a blessed life. Those blessings include working with such phenomenal women as Wendy Lawton, my nonfiction agent along with Janet Grant from Books and Such. Wendy is a woman with vision. She has inspired, cajoled, and encouraged me through every step of this project. When I first mentioned the incident in the airport, it was Wendy who instantly saw the light. This chance encounter was more than happenstance, she insisted, this was a story that needed to be told—more than that, a book that would impact lives. It didn't take me long to catch her vision. Thank you, Wendy, for your faith in me; for your encouragement and support through every step of the process.

Cindy Lambert, my Howard editor, pored endlessly over this manuscript with her magic red pen. Cindy shaped these words and chapters into a work of which I am extremely proud. She is an editor of unmatched insight and heart, and I am fortunate to have worked with her and the entire Howard publishing team.

Nancy Berland, my personal publicist, is a tireless professional who works endlessly long hours to keep my website fresh and current. One of the smartest business decisions I ever made was to hire Nancy. She has blessed my career with her guidance and her friendship.

My office staff, Renate Roth, Wanda Roberts, Heidi Pollard, and Carol Bass, have aided me in innumerable ways. I couldn't manage without them. They are my right hand . . . and my left, both feet, fingers and toes. Thank you for keeping my life organized and sane.

I would be remiss if I didn't mention my husband, children, and eight of the most incredibly talented grandchildren in the universe. I still remember the day more than thirty years ago when I confessed to my family that I wanted to write books. Wayne willing went with me to the office supply store so I could rent my first typewriter. It was a manual because the payment on an electric was more than we could afford. His staunch belief in me hasn't wavered even once despite those fast and furious early rejections.

Oh yes, God has blessed me.

My prayer now is that you will be blessed to by reading this book; that it will open your eyes to the potential blessings that await us when we are generous.

Enjoy.

# Appendix A

*One Simple Act* Reader Questions

**1.** What are some of the things for which you are most grateful? Do you have any "fleas" for which you can begin thanking God? What does it demonstrate when you thank God for the "fleas"?

**2.** In the story of the feeding of the five thousand, the little boy's loaves and fishes were offered to Jesus and he multiplied them to feed the hungry crowds. In your life, what are you own loaves and fishes? What resources do you have?

**3.** Why is encouragement so important? What is the difference between praise and encouragement? Do we overpraise?

**4.** What are some good deeds you've performed? Can you think of small deeds and ways to bless people that would fit into your lifestyle?

**5.** What is it about forgiving that is so difficult? Does forgiving mean you have to forget the offense forever? Does forgiveness guarantee reconciliation?

**6.** How can a person balance the need to be discerning and realistic with playing Pollyanna's Glad Game and finding the good in everyone? Will the Whatever Principle work?

**7.** How can we be "extravagantly generous" with our money? Is it wise to give to others if your own family is struggling financially?

**8.** What is your worst habit as a listener? Your best habit? How do you listen to God?

**9.** How has hospitality changed in this day and age? What have been some of your favorite ways to entertain?

**10**. What ways of dispensing hope are well within your comfort zone? What makes you uncomfortable? Does God expect you to do things that make you uneasy?

**11.** How have you used the Christmas season to point to Jesus? What do you think about Christmas gifts?

**12.** On page 147, Debbie Macomber says that everyone falls into one of four groups: those who have been caregivers, those who are caregivers, those who will be caregivers, and those who will need caregivers. Where do you fall in that continuum? What experiences have you had with caregiving? What advice do you give for those who are called to care for their loved ones?

**13.** How do you prioritize your time? What is the biggest time drain in your life? Are lack of planning and lack of goals keeping you from optimizing your time?

**14.** Why is praying for others so powerful? When two or more people pray together, why does it up the power? Is it dangerous to pray that God make us more generous?

**15.** How do you feel about sharing your faith? How have you been successful? How have you failed miserably? Do you sense any urgency like the pastor on the *Titanic*?

**16.** What does it mean to "have a servant's heart"? What kinds of things have you done to give service to others? What things would you like to do?

# Appendix B

*Some of Debbie Macomber's Favorite Charities*

There are many worthy charities and foundations helping to change the world. These are just a few of Debbie Macomber's favorite. Besides giving regularly to her church, Debbie supports:

## Warm Up America!

Warm Up America! (WUA!) is an organization dedicated to providing warmth and comfort to people who have lost their homes, fled abusive situations, or are being cared for in hospices, shelters, hospitals, and nursing homes. WUA! brings together volunteers who create handmade afghan blankets, clothing and accessories to help those in need.

**www.warmupamerica.com**

## World Vision

World Vision is a Christian humanitarian organization serving close to 100 million people in nearly a hundred countries around the world. Their goal is to help children, families, and communities reach their full potential by tackling the causes of poverty and injustice. World Vision serves all people, regardless of religion, race, ethnicity, or gender.

**www.worldvision.org**

## Point Hope

Point Hope is a charity organization that aspires to be the voice for forgotten children. Started by Debbie's friend, radio personality Delilah, Point Hope's mission is to provide long-lasting solutions that will benefit the forgotten children, and to be their voice, saying "Don't forget about me; I am a person too!"

www.pointhope.org

## Guideposts Foundation

Guideposts Outreach ministry touches millions of lives by bringing the message of faith and hope to people who need God's presence and promises.

www.guideposts.com/outreach

# Notes

### One: Fleas, Footsteps, and Checkout Lanes

1. Corrie ten Boom, *The Hiding Place* (New York: Bantam, 1984).
2. R. A. Emmons and M. E. McCullough, "Highlights from the Research Project on Gratitude and Thankfulness," http://psychology.ucdavis.edu/labs/emmons/.
3. Stephen Post, *Why Good Things Happen to Good People,* excerpted from "The Power of Gratitude," an article in the November 2007 issue of *Guideposts.* Reprinted with permission from *Guideposts.* Copyright © 2007 by Guideposts. All rights reserved. www.guideposts.com.

### Three: Keys, Candy, and Army Men

1. Stephen King, *On Writing* (New York: Pocket Books, 2000), 73–74.

### Five: A Memory, a Guard, and an Outstretched Hand

1. Corrie ten Boom, *Tramp for the Lord* (Fort Washington, Penn.: Christian Literature Crusade, 1974). From *Tramp for the Lord* by Corrie ten Boom, copyright © 1974 by Corrie ten Boom and Jamie Buckingham. Published by CLC Publications, Fort Washington, PA. Used with permission.
2. Martin Luther King, Jr., http://www.quotesandpoem.com/quotes/showquotes/author/martin-luther-king-jr./4706.
3. Søren Kierkegaard, *The Prayers of Søren Kierkegaard* (Chicago: University of Chicago Press, 1996), 21.

### Six: A Coach, a Cough Drop, and a Light Bulb

1. The Haddon Robinson story can be found at http://www.sermonillustrations.com; originally published in the *Christian Medical Society Journal.*
2. Aldous Huxley quoted in Dr. Piero Ferrucci, *The Power of Kindness*: Vivien Reid Ferrucci, trans. (New York, Jeremy P. Tarcher/Penguin, 2007), 11.
4. James Newton, *Uncommon Friends* (New York: Mariner Books, 1989), 19.

### Seven: Point Hope, a Piano Recital, and a House Yet to Come

1. James Kennedy and Jerry Newcombe, *New Every Morning* (Sisters, Or.: Multnomah Books, 2006).
2. The Paderewski story can be found at http://www.sermonillustrations.com.

### Eight: Static, Stories, and Chow-Chow

1. Helen H. Cepero, "Recognizing the Privilege of Listening to Others," *Covenant Companion Magazine,* October 2008.

2. Carver, Johnson, and Friedman, International Listening Association's Website, www.listen.org.

**Nine: Jambalaya, Cupcakes, and the North Platte Canteen**
1. Levi Coffin, *Reminiscences,* published in 1879; text found at History Matters, http://historymatters.gmu.edu/d/6595/.

**Ten: Waiting Rooms, Blossoms, and Letters That Last**
1. C. S. Lewis, *The Last Battle,* Easton Press special ed. (New York: HarperCollins Publishers, 1984), 210.

**Eleven: Glue, Legends, and a Slumber Party**
1. *Gifts in a Bag: Dips; Gifts in a Bag: Rubs and Seasonings;* and *Gifts in a Bag: Hot Drinks* (Waverly, Iowa: G & R Publishing, 2002).

**Twelve: Bread Crumbs, Minnows, and Submarines**
1. Philip Yancey, "The Holy Inefficiency of Henri Nouwen," *Christianity Today,* vol. 40, no. 14, December 9, 1996. Article copyright © 1966 by Philip Yancey.
2. Henry Van Dyke, "Gone from Sight," found at http://www.gutenberg.org/etext/16229.
3. "Tips for Caregivers," National Caregivers Association. Reprinted with permission of the National Family Caregivers Association, Kensington, MD, the nation's only organization for all family caregivers. 1-800-896-3650; http://www.thefamilycaregiver.org.

**Thirteen: A Kingdom, Ten Dollars, and Afghans of Love**
1. Po Bronson, "Where Do We Spend Our Time?" *Time,* October 23, 2006.

**Fourteen: Red Stars, Research, and a Rolex**
1. Richard Foster, *Prayer: Finding the Heart's True Home* (New York: HarperCollins, 1992), 191.
2. Erik Walker Wikstrom, *Simply Pray* (Boston: Skinner House Books, 2005), 42.

**Fifteen: A Question, an Opportunity, and a Conversation Worth Having**
1. John Harper's story can be found online at www.wheaton.edu/bgc/archives/docs/titanic1.htm.

**Sixteen: A Treasure, a Shawl, and a Hymn over the Phone**
1. Jason Zahariades' blog, The Off Ramp, can be found at http://www.theofframp.org/.